DRUG DANGERS

The Dangers of
Alcohol

Peggy J. Parks

ReferencePoint
Press®

San Diego, CA

About the Author

Peggy J. Parks holds a bachelor of science degree from Aquinas College in Grand Rapids, Michigan, where she graduated magna cum laude. An author who has written dozens of educational books on a wide variety of topics for children and young adults, Parks lives in Muskegon, Michigan, a town that she says inspires her writing because of its location on the shores of Lake Michigan.

For more information, contact:
ReferencePoint Press, Inc.
PO Box 27779
San Diego, CA 92198
www.ReferencePointPress.com

LIBRARY OF CONGRESS CATALOGING-IN-PUBLICATION DATA

Names: Parks, Peggy J., 1951- author.
Title: The dangers of alcohol / by Peggy J. Parks.
Description: San Diego, CA : ReferencePoint Press, Inc., 2017. | Series: Drug
  dangers | Includes bibliographical references and index.
Identifiers: LCCN 2015050951 (print) | LCCN 2016006665 (ebook) | ISBN
  9781682820124 (hardback) | ISBN 9781682820131 (epub)
Subjects: LCSH: Alcoholism--Juvenile literature. | Drinking of alcoholic
  beverages--Juvenile literature.
Classification: LCC HV5066 .P37 2017 (print) | LCC HV5066 (ebook) | DDC
  362.292--dc23
LC record available at http://lccn.loc.gov/2015050951

CONTENTS

Chapter 1   4
The Nature of Alcohol Abuse

Chapter 2   16
What Are the Effects of Alcohol?

Chapter 3   29
How Addictive Is Alcohol?

Chapter 4   40
Treatment and Recovery Challenges

Chapter 5   52
How Can Alcohol Abuse Be Prevented?

Source Notes   64

Organizations to Contact   70

For Further Research   74

Index   77

Picture Credits   80

CHAPTER 1: The Nature of Alcohol Abuse

The consumption of alcoholic beverages is common in countries throughout the world, including the United States. According to the National Institute on Alcohol Abuse and Alcoholism (NIAAA), nearly 87 percent of Americans aged eighteen or older have consumed alcohol at some point during their lives, and more than half are current drinkers.

Alcohol has been a focus of research for many years due to its widespread use and the risks associated with its consumption. This has enabled health officials to better understand the effects of long-term alcohol use, the biological and environmental factors that contribute to it, and the prevalence of drinking among different populations, including teenagers.

One of the most comprehensive studies to examine Americans' drinking patterns was published in the April 2015 issue of the *American Journal of Public Health*. Researchers from the Institute for Health Metrics and Evaluation (IHME) in Seattle, Washington, analyzed alcohol use trends in the United States from 2002 to 2012. They found that the prevalence of drinking remained largely unchanged over the ten-year period, but drinking patterns were troubling. "The percentage of people who drink is not changing much," says lead study author Ali Mokdad, "but among drinkers, we are seeing more heavy drinking and more binge drinking. We're going in the wrong direction."[1]

Drinking Levels

When researchers talk about heavy or binge drinking, they are referring to excessive alcohol consumption: amounts that are higher than what health officials recommend. According to the

Centers for Disease Control and Prevention (CDC), a standard drink is equal to 14 grams (1.2 tablespoons) of ethyl alcohol, or ethanol, the chemical name for pure alcohol. In general, this is the amount of alcohol contained in 12 ounces (354.9 ml) of beer, 8 ounces (236.6 ml) of malt liquor, 5 ounces (147.9 ml) of wine, or a 1.5-ounce (44.4 ml) shot of 80-proof hard liquor such as whiskey, gin, rum, or vodka. In terms of pure alcohol content, these drinks are equal, even though the volume of liquid varies widely from drink to drink. "One 12-ounce beer has about the same amount of alcohol as one 5-ounce glass of wine, or 1.5-ounce shot of liquor," says the CDC. "It is the amount of alcohol consumed that affects a person most, not the type of alcoholic drink."[2]

The recommendations for alcohol consumption are not the same for women and men because alcohol affects them differently. Even if a man and woman are of similar height and weight, the woman will typically reach higher concentrations of alcohol in her bloodstream sooner. This is largely because a woman's body contains smaller amounts of alcohol dehydrogenase, a family of enzymes in the liver that help metabolize (break down) alcohol. Also, a woman's body contains less water to dilute alcohol than a man's. Neuroscientist Aaron White likens this to "pouring a shot into a six-ounce glass of Coke rather than a 12-ounce glass."[3] As a result of these differences, health officials define moderate drinking as no more than one drink per day for women and no more than two drinks per day for men.

> "Among drinkers, we are seeing more heavy drinking and more binge drinking. We're going in the wrong direction."[1]
>
> —Ali Mokdad, a professor at the University of Washington's Institute for Health Metrics and Evaluation.

Heavy drinking, as defined by the NIAAA, is consuming fifteen or more drinks per week for men and eight drinks or more per week for women. Binge drinking occurs in spurts: someone consumes enough alcohol in one sitting to bring his or her blood alcohol concentration (BAC) level to 0.08 percent or higher. This typically occurs after a man has five drinks or a woman has had four drinks in about two hours.

Although the volume of alcoholic drinks may vary widely, 12 ounces (354.9 ml) of beer, 8 ounces (236.6 ml) of malt liquor, 5 ounces (147.9 ml) of wine, and a 1.5-ounce (44.4 ml) shot of 80-proof hard liquor all contain the same amount of ethanol, or pure alcohol.

One finding of the April 2015 IHME study was that between 2002 and 2012, heavy drinking among Americans increased more than 17 percent, and binge drinking increased 9 percent. Of particular interest to researchers was that women accounted for most of the growth in heavy and binge drinking. For instance, the prevalence of women who heavily drank jumped more than 38 percent compared with an increase of 18.3 percent among men. Binge drinking rose nearly 19 percent among women, compared with 7.3 percent among men. As NIAAA director George Koob remarks, "Women are drinking more like men, to put it bluntly."[4] Yet even though the rate of alcohol consumption is growing faster among women, the study showed that overall prevalence of drinking remains highest among men.

Regional Variations

The IHME study was the first of its kind to examine trends in alcohol use in counties throughout the United States—and the variances from county to county were striking. In 2012, for instance, overall drinking prevalence ranged from 11 percent in Madison County, Idaho, to 78.7 percent in Falls Church, Virginia. In Nevada's sparsely populated Esmeralda County, 22.4 percent of residents are heavy drinkers compared with 2.4 percent in Hancock County, Tennessee. Other areas with the lowest rates of heavy drinking were Utah County, Utah; Grainger and Johnson Counties, Tennessee; Grant and Dewey Counties, Oklahoma; and Bell County, Kentucky.

The fewest binge drinkers (5.9 percent) in the United States were found in Madison County, Idaho, and the most (36 percent) were in Wisconsin's Menominee County. This is home to the Menominee Indian Reservation, whose residents have had a long and difficult struggle with substance abuse. "This is nothing new to us," says Diane Hietpas, a health educator at the Menominee Tribal Clinic in Keshena, Wisconsin. "People don't understand that this is a symptom of a much larger problem of poverty and trauma. Our people are hurting."[5]

The high prevalence of alcohol abuse in Menominee County is indicative of a problem throughout the entire state. In fact, the IHME study found that Wisconsin is the heaviest-drinking state in the country. According to Julia Sherman, coordinator of the Wisconsin Alcohol Policy Project, the average number of drinks consumed by an individual per year in Wisconsin is 148 drinks more than the national average. Sherman cites three main factors that contribute to Wisconsin's drinking culture. "Two of the biggest ones are the availability of alcohol and the acceptability of alcohol use, the social norms of a community," she says. "A third one that the researchers mentioned is the affordability of alcohol. . . . Alcohol is very cheap in Wisconsin."[6]

Wisconsin is not the only place where alcohol's affordability and acceptance drive high drinking rates. Research has consistently shown that one of the most hard-drinking cities in the United States is Austin, Texas, which is the state capital and home to the University of Texas. Police officer Bob Mitchell, who is with

Austin's drunk-driving unit, sees the problem day after day. "People come here to drink," he says, "and there are a lot of places here to drink. We're known for it."[7] According to state health officials, alcohol consumption in Austin is soaring, with alcohol sales in 2013 totaling $568 million—a 50 percent increase since 2008. Consequently, risky behaviors associated with alcohol are also high there. City records show that arrests for driving while intoxicated (DWI) jumped from forty-nine hundred in 2010 to more than six thousand in 2013. Over that same period, seventy-five people died in drunk-driving crashes, and more than nineteen hundred were injured.

Demographic Disparities

Numerous studies, surveys, and polls have identified certain patterns of alcohol consumption in the United States. One example is a comprehensive July 2015 Gallup poll that showed 64 percent of Americans aged eighteen and older consume alcohol often or occasionally. Of those, the greatest number of drinkers were financially well off; 78 percent of people whose incomes were $75,000 or more drank alcohol (compared with 45 percent of those with incomes of $30,000 or less). An even more profound difference was observed when participants answered questions about current drinking. When asked if they had had one or more alcoholic beverages within the past twenty-four hours, nearly half of upper-income drinkers said yes, compared with only 18 percent of lower-income drinkers.

One conclusion drawn from this disparity is that Americans of higher socioeconomic status have more money to spend and can therefore afford to buy alcohol more often. Also, says Gallup's Jeffrey M. Jones, higher-income people "are more likely to participate in activities that may involve drinking such as dining out at restaurants, going on vacation or socializing with coworkers (given the higher drinking rates among working compared with nonworking Americans)." Although research has not shown a direct connection between drinking and engaging in such activities, Jones says that "such a connection could help explain why upper-income Americans are more likely to drink alcohol than other Americans."[8]

The 2015 Gallup poll also revealed that education is a factor in determining who drinks heavily and who does not. The poll showed that about 18 percent of college graduates sometimes drink more than they should, compared with slightly over half of people who have not graduated from college. "It is unclear," says Jones, "if the education differences on overdrinking truly reflect actual behavior, or perhaps reflect that those with more formal education may be less willing to report a socially undesirable behavior in a public opinion survey."[9]

Other factors were revealed during the July 2015 poll, such as the role religion plays in whether people drink. Nearly half of participants who attend church weekly said they drink alcohol, compared with 69 percent of people who attend church less often or not at all. There were also marked disparities based on gender, with 69 percent of men reporting that they drink compared with 59 percent of women. In addition, racial differences were apparent: 69 percent of non-Hispanic whites reported drinking alcohol compared with 52 percent of nonwhites.

Alcohol Use Disorder

When people are surveyed about their drinking habits, acknowledging that they drink alcohol does not necessarily indicate that they have a drinking problem. The majority of people who drink alcohol are casual or moderate drinkers who do not overindulge. "Seventy percent of Americans drink," says Koob, "and most of them drink responsibly. Alcohol is widely used as a social lubricant, and I don't see anything particularly wrong with that."[10] Koob emphasizes, however, that a significant number of Americans have a drinking problem. This was revealed during an August 2015 NIAAA study, which found that tens of millions of people in the United States struggle with alcohol abuse.

Since 2015 the American Psychiatric Association (APA) has combined all alcohol-related problems into a single condition known as alcohol use disorder (AUD). Within the AUD designation, the extent of someone's alcohol problem is measured on a spectrum of abuse criteria that range from mild to severe. "There are various degrees of this disorder," says Koob. "It could be somebody who's gotten several DUIs. It could be that you just wake up hungover a lot. If you plan to binge over the weekend and miss some classes because of it, then maybe you already have a problem."[11]

> "Seventy percent of Americans drink, and most of them drink responsibly."[10]
>
> —George Koob, director of the National Institute on Alcohol Abuse and Alcoholism.

The severity of an alcohol problem is determined by a person's symptoms, as designated by the APA. These symptoms are being unable to control drinking; wanting to cut down but not being able to do so; spending a lot of time getting alcohol, drinking, and/or recovering from the after-effects of drinking; wanting a drink so badly that one is unable to think about anything else; neglecting work, school, or home obligations; continuing to drink even though it causes trouble with family and friends; giving up activities and hobbies because of drinking; consuming alcohol in situations where it is not safe, such as when driving, swimming, or using machinery; continuing to drink even though it causes feelings of depression and/or anxiety, creates health problems,

Who's Your Driver?

According to the Centers for Disease Control and Prevention, an estimated 10 percent of teenagers have driven after drinking. The good news is that this number has been more than cut in half from 22.3 percent in 1991. What is troubling is that a far greater number of teens are riding with someone else who has been drinking. According to a joint poll by Mothers Against Drunk Driving and State Farm Insurance, 30 percent of teens have been a passenger with a drinking driver at least once during the past year—and 3 percent of those teens have ridden with a drinking driver ten times or more.

The poll was conducted in October 2015 and involved six hundred youth aged fifteen to twenty. Along with asking whether they had ridden with someone who was drinking, teens were asked whether they believe their friends had done so. Sixty percent of the participants said yes, they believed that their friends had been a passenger with a drinking driver during the past year, but only 20 percent intervened to stop them from getting in the car. "Everyone would agree that riding with a drinking driver is not a good idea," says State Farm spokesman Dave Phillips, "but teens are making this choice to do so."

Quoted in Dennis Thompson, "Many Teens Knowingly Ride with Drunk Drivers, Survey Finds," HealthDay, October 22, 2015. http://consumer.healthday.com.

or causes memory blackouts; needing to drink more and more to get the desired effects; and suffering from withdrawal symptoms such as nausea, sweating, a racing heart, and shakiness when not drinking.

According to the NIAAA, a combination of two of these symptoms indicates an alcohol use disorder. Two to three are indicative of mild AUD, four to five signify moderate AUD, and six or more merit a diagnosis of severe AUD. The 2015 NIAAA study revealed that nearly 14 percent of adults met AUD criteria for the previous year, and 29.1 percent met AUD criteria at some time during their lives.

Young Drinkers

Drinking problems also affect teenagers—tens of thousands of them. According to the Substance Abuse and Mental Health

Services Administration (SAMHSA), nearly 700,000 adolescents aged twelve to seventeen suffered from an AUD in 2013. On a positive note, this was a decrease from 2012, when the number of adolescents with an AUD was 855,000. Still, health officials are concerned about the overall prevalence of alcohol use among American youth. "While we're always very happy about these declines," says the SAMHSA's Rich Lucey, "we can't lose sight of the fact that we have approximately 9 million underage drinkers in the country."[12]

To closely monitor trends in abuse of alcohol and other substances, the National Institute on Drug Abuse sponsors a survey called Monitoring the Future (MTF). Each year an estimated forty thousand students in eighth, tenth, and twelfth grades at schools throughout the United States answer questions about their health-risk behaviors. The 2014 survey (published in February 2015) revealed that an alarming number of teens were drinking alcohol to the point of intoxication. Specifically, more than 23 percent of high school seniors, 11.2 percent of sophomores, and nearly 3 percent of eighth-graders reported getting drunk within the past month.

> "We can't lose sight of the fact that we have approximately 9 million underage drinkers in the country."[12]
>
> —Rich Lucey, special assistant to the director of the Substance Abuse and Mental Health Services Administration.

Especially disturbing to health officials is the number of youth who binge drink (consume five or more drinks in a row during a certain period of time). According to the research group Child Trends, the practice is "the most common form of alcohol consumption among adolescents."[13] The 2014 MTF survey revealed that 4.1 percent of eighth-graders, 12.6 percent of tenth-graders, and 19.4 percent of high school seniors binge drank at some point in the two weeks prior to the survey.

Binge drinking is also a well-known and widespread problem among college and university students throughout the United States. SAMHSA research has shown that about 60 percent of college students drink alcohol, and nearly 40 percent of those have participated in binge drinking. Drinking rates among college students have remained relatively steady for the past decade, largely

Teen Drinking Is Declining

Although health officials are concerned about the high number of young people who drink alcohol, they welcomed the encouraging news that between 2002 and 2013, alcohol use and binge drinking declined among young Americans aged twelve to twenty.

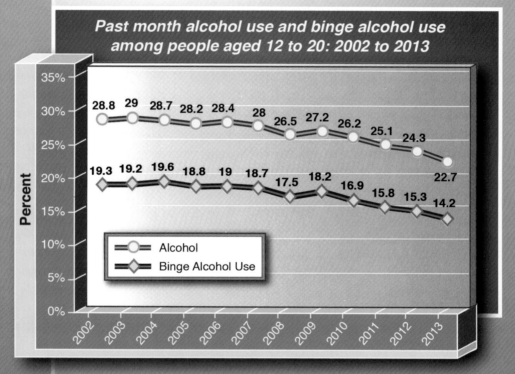

Source: Substance Abuse and Mental Health Services Administration, "Underage Drinking Declined Between 2002 and 2013," June 11, 2015. www.samhsa.gov.

because many students regard drinking as part of going to college. "Drinking at college has become a ritual that students often see as an integral part of their higher education experience," says the NIAAA. "Many students come to college with established drinking habits, and the college environment can exacerbate the problem."[14]

This was the case for Ben Yeager, who is now a freelance writer living in New York City. Throughout high school he drank heavily to the point of blacking out, and he continued to drink even after crashing his mother's car and being arrested for DWI.

Heavy-Drinking Jobs

Substance abuse costs the US economy billions of dollars each year in lost productivity, workplace accidents and injuries, employee absenteeism, and increased illness. To determine which industries and occupations were associated with the heaviest drinking and drug use, researchers from the Substance Abuse and Mental Health Services Administration analyzed federal data from 2003 to 2012. They found that, on average, nearly 9 percent of full-time workers aged eighteen to sixty-four were heavy drinkers. Breaking the data down by industry allowed researchers to see the wide discrepancies from one occupation to another. For instance, the highest rates of heavy drinking were among those who work in the mining industry: nearly 18 percent of these workers drank heavily. Close behind the mining industry was construction, at 16.5 percent of employees. Accommodations and food services, arts and entertainment, and utilities workers rounded out the top five industries with the heaviest drinking.

The lowest number of heavy-drinking employees worked in the fields of health care, social assistance, and educational services, each of which had less than one-third the prevalence of mining and construction. Workers in public administration (government employees), finance and insurance, and professional/scientific/technical services were also low on the list for prevalence of heavy drinking.

When Yeager entered college, he was ready to enjoy the freedom of drinking whenever he wanted to. "To me, college seemed like a great place to party," he says. "After my first night as a freshman, I woke up in an Adirondack chair in the middle of the college quad, freezing, wet with dew and with no idea how I'd gotten there or what I'd done the night before. What would become regular blackouts amused my peers and became fodder for cafeteria mythmaking, an unwavering celebration of college excess."[15]

Drinking and Driving

One of the most dangerous by-products of the alcohol abuse problem in the United States is the high prevalence of people who drink and drive. According to an August 2015 report by CDC researchers, behavioral risk surveys have shown that more than

4 million adults have driven drunk one or more times within thirty days of being surveyed. Binge drinkers are most likely to drive drunk, and men, by far, are the greatest drunk-driving offenders; the CDC report shows that 80 percent of drunk-driving instances involve male drivers.

For an April 2014 report, the financial news and opinion group 24/7 Wall St. analyzed data from the Foundation for the Advancement of Alcohol Responsibility. The group identified and ranked the US states that have the worst problems with drunk driving. One of these was North Dakota, which had the highest beer consumption in the United States, the third highest number of underage drinkers, and the largest increase in drunk-driving deaths of any state in the country. Another problematic state was Montana, which was among the states with the highest youth consumption of alcohol and the highest rates of binge drinking among youth. "Sadly," says 24/7 Wall St.'s Vince Calio, "for every 100,000 people in the state, 3.8 underage residents were killed in drunk driving accidents, second highest in the country."[16] Following closely behind Montana is South Carolina, which had nearly eighteen thousand drunk-driving arrests in 2012, one of the highest rates in the United States.

> "I woke up in an Adirondack chair in the middle of the college quad, freezing, wet with dew and with no idea how I'd gotten there or what I'd done the night before."[15]
>
> —Ben Yeager, freelance writer.

Harsh Realities

As troubling as drunk driving is, a February 2015 National Highway Transportation Safety Administration survey revealed some hopeful news. The number of drivers with alcohol in their system has declined by 30 percent since 2007 and by more than 75 percent since the first of such surveys was conducted in 1973. Promising observations have also been made in other areas, such as the steady decline in alcohol use among youth and the decreasing number of high school students who binge drink. As hopeful as these factors are, however, millions of Americans, from teenagers to older adults, continue to abuse alcohol on a regular basis.

CHAPTER 2: What Are the Effects of Alcohol?

Alcohol affects people in different ways depending on a variety of factors. These include gender, body fat and muscle mass, how someone feels while drinking, his or her experience with alcohol, and how quickly the alcohol is consumed. Chugging beer, for example, is more likely to cause intoxication than sipping a glass of wine over the course of an hour. When someone drinks, about 20 percent of the alcohol goes directly into the bloodstream from the stomach lining. The rest moves into the small intestine and enters the bloodstream from there. "Once in the bloodstream," says a Rutgers University health publication, "alcohol circulates throughout the body and it can begin to affect you within several minutes."[17]

After one or two drinks, a person typically feels warm and relaxed, and perhaps more sociable than usual. If within a short time the person has three drinks, his or her motor coordination, meaning the use of muscles, hands, and feet, will be affected. This is the point at which people may lose their balance and stumble or fall down. "Although you may feel you can drive a car, it is very risky," says the Rutgers publication. "Speech is also impaired and you can become noisy and possibly aggressive. The more alcohol you drink, the greater the effect on your behavior."[18]

Blank Spaces

One of the risks for someone who drinks too much, too fast is a state of alcohol-induced amnesia known as a blackout. The term is often used interchangeably with *passing out,* but is not the same. Someone who blacks out is not unconscious; he or she is fully awake but will not remember conversations or behaviors because the brain is unable to create memories of them. "Your brain will have no imprint of these activities, almost as if they didn't happen," says Sarah Hepola, author of the 2015 memoir *Blackout: Remembering the Things I Drank to Forget*. "Once memories are lost in a blackout, they can't be coaxed back. Simple logic: Information that wasn't stored cannot be retrieved."[19] In her book, Hepola candidly discusses her years-long alcohol problem. The book gets its name from her focus on the innumerable times she drank so heavily that she blacked out.

Neuroscientist Aaron White is one of America's foremost experts on alcohol's effects on the brain and body, and one of his areas of expertise is the blackout. He says that when people black out, they are much more likely than usual to engage in risky behaviors. These include getting behind the wheel of a car, walking in unsafe neighborhoods, or having unprotected sex. Women are more likely to black out than men—and when they do, their risk of being sexually assaulted soars. According to White, this violent crime is much more likely to occur when a woman has blacked out than when she is fully cognizant and aware of her surroundings and behavior. "When men are in a blackout, they do things to the world," says White. "When women are in a blackout, things are done to them."[20]

> "When men are in a blackout, they do things to the world. When women are in a blackout, things are done to them."[20]
>
> —Aaron White, a neuroscientist and senior adviser to the director of the NIAAA.

According to the NIAAA, blackouts typically occur when someone's BAC is around .20. That is more than twice the legal limit for driving in all fifty states and a level that is considered highly intoxicated as well as dangerous. "We think about 50 percent of people will die at a .35," says White. "So you're getting up there."[21] Scientists have identified two specific types of blackouts: the en bloc and the fragmentary. When someone has experienced an en bloc blackout, whole blocks of time, such as an entire afternoon or evening, are missing from his or her memory. More common is a fragmentary blackout, in which an individual has lost bits and pieces of time, such as having spotty memories of a particular occasion.

Why BAC Matters

How drinking affects people depends on how much alcohol is in their blood, which is measured by their blood alcohol concentration (BAC). As shown here, the higher the BAC, the more incapacitated someone typically becomes.

Blood Alcohol Concentration	Typical Effects
.02% About 2 alcoholic drinks	• Some loss of judgment • Relaxation • Slight body warmth • Altered mood
.05% About 3 alcoholic drinks	• Exaggerated behavior • May have loss of small-muscle control (e.g., focusing one's eyes) • Impaired judgment • Usually good feeling • Lowered alertness • Release of inhibition
.08% About 4 alcoholic drinks	• Muscle coordination becomes poor (e.g., balance, speech, vision, reaction time, and hearing) • Harder to detect danger • Judgment, self-control, reasoning, and memory are impaired
.10% About 5 alcoholic drinks	• Clear deterioration of reaction time and control • Slurred speech, poor coordination, and slowed thinking
.15% About 7 alcoholic drinks	• Far less muscle control than normal • Vomiting may occur (unless this level is reached slowly or a person has developed a tolerance for alcohol) • Major loss of balance

Source: Centers for Disease Control and Prevention, "Effects of Blood Alcohol Concentration (BAC)," August 17, 2015. www.cdc.gov.

With either type of blackout, the memories are gone because the brain never created them in the first place.

Anyone who drinks excessively can black out, but some people are at higher risk than others. College students are especially vulnerable, according to White, because of their penchant for binge drinking. "Alcohol is more likely to cause a blackout when it gets into your body, and therefore your brain, fast," he says. "It catches the memory circuits off guard and shuts them down."[22]

Disrupted Brain Chemistry

Many people who drink heavily or binge drink slur their words when trying to speak, lose their balance and stumble, feel nauseated, black out, and possibly even pass out. This is due to alcohol's effect on brain chemistry, meaning the intricate, complex maze of nerve cells (neurons), chemicals, and processes that enable the brain to work. "The physical structure of the brain remains constant," says neuroscientist Joshua Gowin, "but the addition of a tiny chemical drastically alters brain function and ultimately behavior."[23]

The key to brain function is its neurons, which continuously send messages to each other via rapid-fire electrochemical signals. "Every millisecond of every day, a remarkable string of events occurs in the brain," says the Society for Neuroscience. "Billions of brain cells called neurons transmit signals to each other. . . . It is an extremely fast and efficient process—one central to everything the brain does, including learning, memorizing, planning, reasoning, and enabling movement."[24] Signals are passed from one neuron to another across tiny gaps between neurons called synapses. This process is facilitated by chemical messengers known as neurotransmitters, of which there are two primary types: excitatory and inhibitory. Excitatory neurotransmitters stimulate the brain and other parts of the nervous system. Inhibitory neurotransmitters have a calming effect, helping create balance in brain chemistry by preventing some neurons from sending messages to others.

According to the NIAAA, heavy alcohol consumption can throw "the delicate balance of neurotransmitters off course."[25] This may cause the chemicals to relay information too slowly, which leads to drowsiness. Likewise, alcohol-related disruptions to neurotransmitter balance can cause mood and behavioral changes, including depression, agitation, memory loss, and possibly seizures.

Brain research has shown that certain neurotransmitters are more vulnerable than others to the effects of alcohol. One example is glutamate, the brain's main excitatory neurotransmitter. When working properly, glutamate increases brain activity and energy levels and also boosts memory and learning. But alcohol interferes with glutamate's normal function by suppressing its release. At the same time, alcohol leads to excessive amounts of the inhibitory neurotransmitter gamma-aminobutyric acid (GABA), which amplifies its sedative effects. Thus, by suppressing the effects of glutamate and amplifying the effects of GABA, alcohol effectively derails two key brain systems.

When alcohol disrupts the balance of neurotransmitters, the brain tries to compensate for the disruption. "Neurotransmitters adapt to create balance in the brain despite the presence of alcohol," says the NIAAA. "But making these adaptations can have negative results."[26] A potentially dangerous effect of neurotransmitter imbalance is withdrawal, which occurs when someone abruptly stops drinking. Symptoms of alcohol withdrawal include anxiety, profuse sweating, trembling, nausea, and vomiting, among others. Severe withdrawal can result in seizures, uncontrollable trembling, hallucinations, and a serious medical condition known as hypertension (high blood pressure).

"We used to think that brain development was done by the time you're a teenager. Now we know that's not true."[27]

—Lorena Siqueira, a pediatrician and researcher from Miami, Florida.

Risks to the Still-Developing Brain

People of all ages can suffer from the harmful effects of alcohol, but its effects on the brain are more profound in adolescents than in adults. This is because the adolescent brain is not fully developed. "We used to think that brain development was done by the time you're a teenager," says Lorena Siqueira, a pediatrician and

A Deadly Risk

More than ten thousand people in the United States were killed in alcohol-impaired driving crashes in 2013. Put another way, every day almost thirty people die in motor vehicle crashes that involve an alcohol-impaired driver. Car crashes are the leading cause of death for teens, and about one-fourth of those crashes involve an underage drinking driver. On average, two out of three people will be involved in a drunk-driving crash during their lifetime. "Alcohol, drugs and driving simply do not go together," says the National Council on Alcoholism and Drug Dependence (NCADD). "Driving requires a person's attentiveness and the ability to make quick decisions on the road, to react to changes in the environment and execute specific, often difficult maneuvers behind the wheel. When drinking alcohol, using drugs, or being distracted for any reason, driving becomes dangerous—and potentially lethal!"

Alcohol impairs driving skills in numerous ways. It slows down the central nervous system, which means that normal brain function is disrupted. Alcohol can impair vision as well as affect someone's cognitive (information-processing) skills and hand-eye coordination. It induces feelings of drowsiness and reduces reaction time. "When alcohol is consumed," says the NCADD, "many of the skills that safe driving requires—such as judgment, concentration, comprehension, coordination, visual acuity, and reaction time—become impaired." Overall, drinking and driving dramatically increases the risk of car crashes, injury, and death.

National Council on Alcoholism and Drug Dependence, "Driving While Impaired," June 26, 2015. https://ncadd.org.

researcher from Miami, Florida. "Now we know that's not true."[27] Years of research have shown that the brain develops from the back to the front. The prefrontal cortex, which is at the front of the head just behind the forehead, is the last part to fully develop. This part of the brain controls such functions as reasoning, problem solving, impulse control, and decision making. Scientists emphasize that teens are prone to risky behaviors (such as drinking) in large part because the prefrontal cortex is still a work in progress.

Because of the brain changes taking place during adolescence, the teen brain responds to alcohol differently than the adult brain. For example, brain circuitry involved in memory is more vulnerable to alcohol during adolescence; thus, alcohol use can more profoundly impair memory in teens than in adults. Another difference is that, for reasons not well understood, teens tend to be less sensitive than adults to alcohol's sedative qualities. According to the Johns Hopkins Bloomberg School of Public Health, sedation (meaning a relaxed, sleepy state) is one of the ways the body protects itself when someone drinks alcohol "since it is impossible to keep drinking once asleep or passed out." Research has shown that teenagers are able to stay awake longer with a high blood alcohol level than can older drinkers. Teens who drink may not see this as a problem, but it is—a potentially dangerous one. Johns Hopkins researchers explain that "this biological difference allows teens to drink more, thereby exposing themselves to greater cognitive impairment and perhaps brain damage from alcohol poisoning."[28]

The adolescent brain is also vulnerable to the effects of binge drinking, which can cause long-lasting brain damage. Scientists have learned that heavy alcohol use during adolescence could permanently change the way the brain functions, meaning damages are irreversible. Studies by Duke University researchers, for instance, have shown that adolescent animals exposed to alcohol grew into adults with impaired memory. To further explore this phenomenon, in 2015 Duke researcher Mary-Louise Risher led a study in which young rodents were fed enough alcohol to bring their BACs to levels that equated those of binge-drinking teens. After sixteen days, the rodents were allowed to grow without any exposure to alcohol.

When the rodents reached adulthood, Risher's group measured the alcohol's effects on their brain cells. They did this by attaching small electrical stimuli to each rodent's hippocampus, the region of the brain that controls memory and learning. They found that neurons in the creatures' brains were more immature than normal and did not function properly. Thus, even though alcohol exposure stopped before the rodents were adults, it had caused permanent brain damage. "In the eyes of the law, once people reach the age of 18, they are considered adult," says Risher, "but the brain continues to mature and refine all the way into the mid-20s. It's important for young people to know that when they drink heavily during this period of development, there could be changes occurring that have a lasting impact on memory and other cognitive functions."[29]

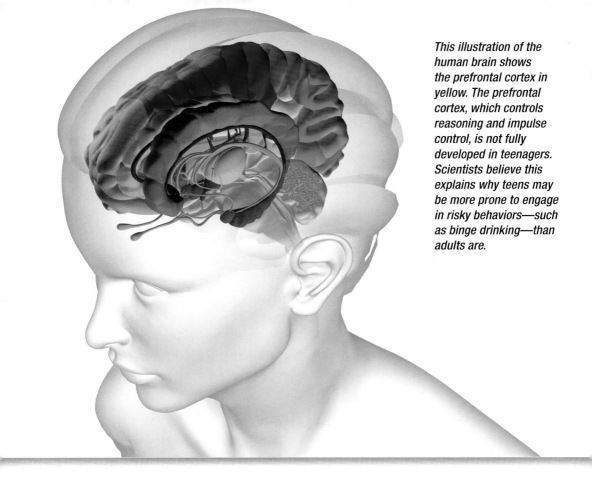

This illustration of the human brain shows the prefrontal cortex in yellow. The prefrontal cortex, which controls reasoning and impulse control, is not fully developed in teenagers. Scientists believe this explains why teens may be more prone to engage in risky behaviors—such as binge drinking—than adults are.

The Perils of Teen Drinking

Along with risks to brains that are not fully developed, teens who drink alcohol expose themselves to innumerable other dangers. "Drinking levels that may cause little or no problem for adults may be dangerous for adolescents," says Siqueira and her colleague Vincent C. Smith. By far, the greatest risk to young people is posed by binge drinking. In a September 2015 report, Siqueira and Smith provided a detailed description of these risks. In the United States, they write, 50 percent of all adolescent head injuries are associated with alcohol consumption. Also, because alcohol impairs judgment, teens who binge drink are more likely to drink and drive, ride in a car with an impaired driver, and/or partake in other behaviors that can lead to serious injury or death. "Alcohol use is involved in each of the major causes of mortality in adolescents such as accidents, suicides, and homicides,"[30] Siqueira and Smith explain.

Emergency vehicles arrive at the scene of a motor vehicle accident. The impaired judgment that results from binge drinking makes teens more likely to drink and drive or ride with an impaired driver, actions that greatly increase their likelihood of experiencing a serious car crash.

Adolescent binge drinking is also closely connected with risky teen sexual activity, including earlier sexual involvement and more sexual partners. Higher rates of unwanted pregnancy have been associated with adolescent alcohol use, as has a higher likelihood of sexually transmitted infections. In addition, say Siqueira and Smith, "Adolescents are at higher risk of becoming the victims of unwanted sexual activity, actual or attempted forced sexual activity, and sexual victimization when binge drinking."[31]

Alcohol Poisoning

One of the most dangerous risks for people of all ages who drink excessively is alcohol overdose, or alcohol poisoning. According to the NIAAA, alcohol poisoning occurs when there is so much alcohol in the bloodstream that areas of the brain responsible for basic life-support functions—such as breathing, heart rate, and temperature control—begin to shut down. An individual suffering from alcohol poisoning may have an extremely low body temperature and clammy skin. Other symptoms include confusion, trouble staying awake, vomiting, seizures, breathing problems, a slow heart rate, and dulled responses, such as no gag reflex (the gag reflex prevents choking).

Whether drinkers are asleep or awake, alcohol in the stomach and small intestine enters the bloodstream and circulates throughout the body. Thus, BAC can continue to rise even if someone is unconscious—creating a potentially deadly situation. "It is dangerous to assume that an unconscious person will be fine by sleeping it off," says the NIAAA. "Alcohol acts as a depressant, hindering signals in the brain that control automatic responses such as the gag reflex. Alcohol also can irritate the stomach, causing vomiting. With no gag reflex, a person who drinks to the point of passing out is in danger of choking on vomit, which, in turn, could lead to death by asphyxiation."[32] Even if the drinker survives, such asphyxiation deprives the brain of oxygen, which can lead to long-lasting brain damage.

Shelby Allen, a seventeen-year-old girl from Redding, California, died of alcohol poisoning in December 2008. It was the first night of Christmas vacation, and Allen and her friends wanted to celebrate the upcoming holidays. For some reason, Allen had set a goal for herself to drink fifteen shots of vodka, and that was what she intended to do. "We all told her it was a bad idea, but she was determined to make that her goal,"[33] says Allen's best friend, Alyssa.

> "It is dangerous to assume that an unconscious person will be fine by sleeping it off."[32]
>
> —National Institute on Alcohol Abuse and Alcoholism, an agency of the National Institutes of Health and the largest funder of alcohol research in the world.

The two girls were together at another friend's house, where the mood was celebratory and alcohol was plentiful. As Allen continued to drink shot after shot of vodka, she chronicled her progress in text messages to friends, with the wording growing sloppier and more incoherent as Allen grew increasingly drunker. One recipient of a text, concerned about Allen's obvious intoxication, texted her back and told her to slow down, but Allen kept drinking. The next morning she was found slumped over in a bathroom and not breathing. When the paramedics arrived, Allen had a weak pulse but they could not save her. She was pronounced dead at

9:40 a.m. on December 20, 2008, and she later was determined to have a BAC of 0.33.

As tragic as such stories are, they are rare; few teens die from alcohol poisoning. According to a January 2015 report by CDC researchers, an average of 2,220 people older than fifteen died of alcohol poisoning each year from 2010 to 2012. Nearly 77 percent of the victims were aged thirty-five to sixty-four, and only 5 percent were teens or young adults.

Liver Damage

People who drink heavily over a long period of time can do extensive harm to their bodies. Although this includes virtually every vital organ, the liver suffers the most. The liver performs invaluable functions, such as filtering harmful substances out of blood from the digestive tract before passing the blood to the rest of the body. The liver also detoxifies chemicals, metabolizes drugs, and makes proteins that are essential for blood clotting and other vital functions.

According to Alexis Janda, Georgetown University's associate director of health promotion and prevention, normally functioning liver cells use fatty acids as fuel. Excess fatty acids are converted into a type of fat called triglycerides, which are then routed through the bloodstream to other tissues of the body. When alcohol is in the blood, however, liver cells must first metabolize that, which allows large amounts of fatty acids to accumulate in the liver. This results in a disease known as steatosis, or fatty liver.

The American Liver Foundation cites fatty liver disease as one of the main types of alcohol-related diseases of the liver. Many heavy drinkers suffer from the condition, which is considered the earliest stage of alcohol-related liver disease. Another of these diseases is alcoholic hepatitis, which is characterized by fat deposition in liver cells, inflammation, and mild scarring of the liver. Alcoholic hepatitis may be mild or severe, and according to the American Liver Foundation, up to 35 percent of heavy drinkers develop it. "Mild alcoholic

"Severe alcoholic hepatitis may occur suddenly and lead to serious complications including liver failure and death."[34]

—American Liver Foundation, which promotes education, support, and research for the prevention and cure of liver disease.

"A Tonic and a Poison"

In a July 2015 poll, 17 percent of respondents said they believed that moderate drinking (one or two drinks a day) was good for their health, with the remainder saying that it either had no effect on health or was harmful. "Throughout the 10,000 or so years that humans have been drinking fermented beverages, they've also been arguing about their merits and demerits," say the authors of a Harvard T.H. Chan School of Public Health article. "The debate still simmers today, with a lively back-and-forth over whether alcohol is good for you or bad for you." The authors add that both perspectives have merit. "It's safe to say that alcohol is both a tonic and a poison. The difference lies mostly in the dose."

Dozens of studies have shown that moderate drinking can reduce the risk of death from cardiovascular causes, including heart attack, ischemic (clot-caused) stroke, and peripheral vascular disease, in which narrowed arteries reduce blood flow to the limbs. Another benefit of moderate alcohol use is its association with a lowered risk of gallstones and type 2 diabetes. Also, there are social and psychological benefits to moderate drinking. "A drink before a meal can improve digestion or offer a soothing respite at the end of a stressful day," the Harvard authors write. They go on to say that the key is to drink in moderation, which "sits at the point at which the health benefits of alcohol clearly outweigh the risks."

Harvard T.H. Chan School of Public Health, "Alcohol: Balancing Risks and Benefits." www.hsph.harvard.edu.

hepatitis may be reversed with abstinence," the foundation explains. "Severe alcoholic hepatitis may occur suddenly and lead to serious complications including liver failure and death."[34]

The most advanced form of alcohol-induced liver disease, known as cirrhosis, is characterized by severe scarring and disruption of normal liver structure: soft, healthy liver tissue is displaced by hard scar tissue. According to the American Liver Foundation, between 10 and 20 percent of heavy drinkers develop cirrhosis. As the disease progresses, scar tissue continues to build up, making it extremely difficult for the liver to function. Cirrhosis is life-threatening; without treatment and abstinence from alcohol, the disease is fatal.

Other Health Dangers

Another risk for people who regularly drink alcohol, especially heavy drinkers, is cancer. Numerous studies have shown that the more someone drinks, the more he or she increases the chances of developing certain types of cancer. One type that is closely connected to drinking is breast cancer. According to the Susan G. Komen organization, a pooled analysis of data from more than fifty studies found that for each alcoholic drink consumed per day, the relative risk of breast cancer increased by about 7 percent. Women who had two to three drinks per day had a 20 percent higher risk of breast cancer.

Other types of cancer associated with alcohol consumption include cancer of the mouth, the esophagus (the tube connecting the throat to the stomach), the pharynx (the membrane-lined cavity behind the nose and mouth that connects to the esophagus), the larynx (voice box), the liver, and the colon. "Scientists are still trying to figure out exactly how and why alcohol can promote cancer,"[35] says the NIAAA, adding that this is a high priority for ongoing scientific research.

Alcohol can also be damaging to the heart. While some research has shown moderate drinking (especially of red wine) to have cardiovascular benefits, long-term heavy alcohol use can weaken the heart muscle, causing a condition known as alcoholic cardiomyopathy. "A weakened heart droops and stretches and cannot contract effectively," says the NIAAA. "As a result, it cannot pump enough blood to sufficiently nourish the organs. In some cases, this blood flow shortage causes severe damage to organs and tissues . . . [and] can even lead to heart failure."[36] The NIAAA goes on to say that binge drinkers are nearly 40 percent more likely to suffer a stroke than people who never binge drink, and they are also more vulnerable to developing high blood pressure.

The Innumerable Risks of Heavy Drinking

From blackouts to disruptions in brain chemistry, cancer, and vital organ damage, alcohol can wreak havoc on the body. Many experts say that the key is moderation: that the problems associated with alcohol stem not so much from the substance itself but from drinking far more than is healthy or safe.

CHAPTER 3: How Addictive Is Alcohol?

Erica, a young woman from Los Angeles, California, is a professional designer and calligrapher as well as a recovered alcoholic. She started drinking when she was in college and made a concerted effort to pace herself. "I placed parameters around when I was allowed to drink," she says, "generally limiting it to certain days and sometimes even taking a break for a month at a time to check that my drinking was under control." By the time Erica was in her mid-twenties, however, she had lost the ability to control how much she drank. "My drinking was making life unmanageable," she says. "And yet, I was completely blind to my problem." Erica drank regularly at home, but she did her heaviest drinking while she was out with her friends. "Once out," she says, "one drink would turn into seven, eight, nine. I drank to celebrate, I drank to escape, I drank to manage the every day."[37]

Even though on some level she knew the truth, Erica told herself over and over that she did not have a problem. She was convinced that she could cut back on drinking if only she could muster the self-discipline. "I thought I couldn't be an alcoholic," she says. Erica grew increasingly desperate to convince herself that her drinking was normal because she found the idea of living without alcohol unthinkable. "My relationship with alcohol had become an addiction," she says, "and addictions, it turns out, are blind spots."[38]

> "One drink would turn into seven, eight, nine. I drank to celebrate, I drank to escape, I drank to manage the every day."[37]
>
> —Erica, a designer from Los Angeles, California, who recovered from alcoholism.

Beyond Problem Drinking

Erica is one of millions of people who, over time, have progressed from drinking in moderation to becoming addicted to alcohol. This is a condition known as alcohol dependence or, as it is more often called, alcoholism. Over the years, after innumerable studies examining how drinkers are affected by alcohol, most scientists are convinced that alcoholism is a chronic, complex disease of the brain. "Addiction is a disease, just like asthma, diabetes and heart disease," says Richard G. Soper, a psychiatrist from Nashville, Tennessee, who specializes in addiction medicine. Soper says that illicit drugs and alcohol activate reward systems in the brain, which in turn cause people to feel compelled to keep using the substances. Soper explains that how alcohol affects people who drink varies because everyone has a unique tolerance. "The effects of drugs and/or alcohol are individually specific,"[39] he says.

Addiction to alcohol has only recently come to be viewed as a disease. Prior to the early to mid-twentieth century, the inability to quit drinking was largely viewed as a character defect or a moral failing. Barron H. Lerner, a professor of medicine at the New York University School of Medicine, explains that "organizations like the Women's Christian Temperance Union promoted the notion that 'drunks' and 'sots' were sinners too weak to stand up to 'demon rum,' beer and other alcoholic beverages." Viewpoints about alcohol began to change during the 1930s. Scientists and physicians began to theorize that alcoholism might be a physical ailment with causes that had little or nothing to do with morals. One notable development during that time was the founding of Alcoholics Anonymous (AA), which Lerner says played a pivotal role in the shift in perspective about alcoholism. "Although it did not specifically term alcoholism a disease," says Lerner, "A.A. popularized this notion."[40]

"The alcoholic is frequently in the grip of a powerful craving for alcohol, a need that can feel as strong as the need for food or water."[41]

—National Council on Alcoholism and Drug Dependence, a leading advocacy organization that addresses alcoholism and drug dependence.

Even though alcoholism is much better understood today compared with the past, there are still numerous misconceptions about it. One is that when someone's drinking has spiraled out of control, this must somehow be due to a lack of willpower. "Most alcoholics can't just 'use a little willpower' to stop drinking," says the NCADD. The disease

An intoxicated teen rests his head on a bar. In the past, people who were unable to control their drinking were seen as lacking willpower, but experts today say that much more than willpower is needed for a person to cope with the disease of alcoholism.

of alcoholism is much more powerful than that. "Alcoholism has little to do with what kind of alcohol one drinks, how long one has been drinking, or even exactly how much alcohol one consumes. But it has a great deal to do with a person's uncontrollable need for alcohol. . . . The alcoholic is frequently in the grip of a powerful craving for alcohol, a need that can feel as strong as the need for food or water."[41]

Alcoholism manifests in four distinct characteristics: cravings, or strong (sometimes overwhelming) urges to drink; loss of control, meaning loss of the ability to stop once drinking has begun; physical dependence, or a need so great that abstinence leads to withdrawal symptoms; and tolerance, or the need to drink greater amounts of alcohol in order to feel the desired effects. "When the brain is exposed to alcohol, it may become tolerant— or insensitive—to alcohol's effects," says the NIAAA. "Thus, as a person continues to drink heavily, he or she may need more alcohol than before to become intoxicated. As tolerance increases, drinking may escalate, putting a heavy drinker at risk for a number of health problems."[42]

The Adaptive Brain

Because alcohol is legal (for adults to purchase), widely acceptable, relatively easy to obtain, and extraordinarily popular, many people do not think of it as a drug—but it is. Alcohol's primary ingredient, ethanol, is an intoxicating substance. Thus, just as illicit drugs (heroin, cocaine, or marijuana) alter someone's mood and behavior, the same is true of alcohol, and people can become addicted to it just as they can other drugs. "Alcoholism is

The Firewater Myth

It is well known that substance abuse, including alcoholism, is disproportionately high among Native American populations. Researchers have identified contributing factors, including the dramatically higher rates of poverty among Native Americans, a widespread prevalence of racism against native peoples, and a history of trauma that spans generations. Another theory, one that is highly controversial, is that genes are responsible for the soaring alcoholism rate among Native Americans.

The reason this idea is so hotly debated is that it is rooted in a discredited theory called the Firewater Myth, with *Firewater* derived from Native American words for "alcohol." The theory goes like this, says journalist Maia Szalavitz: "Europeans introduced Native Americans to alcohol, which they were genetically unprepared to handle. That happenstance led to alcoholism rates that are around twice as high as those seen in whites. . . . In this view, colonization didn't make conquered people susceptible to heavy drinking—genes did."

In February 2013 neuroscientists Cindy L. Ehlers and Ian R. Gizer released a study that examined the possible genetic components for substance dependence in Native Americans. After an in-depth analysis of scientific literature, they concluded that there was a substantial genetic connection with substance dependence, including alcoholism—but the risk was no greater than for other ethnic groups. Ehlers and Gizer determined that the high rates of substance dependence seen among members of Native American tribes is likely a combination of genetic factors combined with environmental risk factors such as exposure to trauma, early onset of substance use, and environmental hardships.

Maia Szalavitz, "No, Native Americans Aren't Genetically More Susceptible to Alcoholism," The Verge, October 2, 2015. www.theverge.com.

an addiction—it's just one type of addiction," says John Sharp, a psychiatrist who specializes in addiction medicine. "When you break out the specific things that someone who is suffering from alcoholism contends with—impaired control, preoccupation with a drug, using despite adverse consequences, distortions in thinking, most notably along the lines of denial—they are no different from any other type of addict."[43]

Through ongoing brain studies, scientists have learned that the key to alcoholism is how significantly alcohol can change the brain over time. To function normally, and keep the body's functions properly regulated, the brain must maintain a precise balance of its neurotransmitters. Alcohol disrupts this process by interfering with normal brain chemistry. "Just as a heavy weight can tip a scale," says the NIAAA, "alcohol intoxication can alter the delicate balance among different types of neurotransmitter chemicals and can lead to drowsiness, loss of coordination, and euphoria—hallmarks of alcohol intoxication."[44]

As the brain continues to be exposed to alcohol over a long period of time, it has to work even harder to keep its chemistry in balance. It begins adapting to the chemical changes caused by alcohol in order to compensate for these disturbances. In an effort to restore its proper chemical balance, the function of some neurotransmitters begins to change. This is the brain's way of trying to perform normally despite the presence of alcohol. Scientists believe that these long-term chemical changes are what ultimately lead to alcoholism. "Repeatedly abusing drugs or alcohol permanently rewires the brain," says the NCADD. "Every time a person abuses alcohol or drugs, it strengthens the wiring associated with these substances, and the more one chases the effect of alcohol and drugs, the greater the chance of developing an addiction."[45] As someone continues to drink heavily, this can lead to profound changes in brain chemistry. These changes can make the person believe that drinking is the only way to avoid the unbearable discomfort associated with withdrawal.

> "Repeatedly abusing drugs or alcohol permanently rewires the brain."[45]
>
> —National Council on Alcoholism and Drug Dependence, a leading advocacy organization that addresses alcoholism and drug dependence.

A Theory Proved

For decades scientists have known that alcohol profoundly affects the brain, but exactly how this happens has been unclear. One important study that revealed alcohol's addictive properties was conducted in 2012 by researchers from the Ernest Gallo Clinic and Research Center at the University of California, San Francisco. The study examined the processes that occur in the brain when someone drinks alcohol.

The study involved twenty-five participants, including thirteen heavy drinkers and a control group of twelve others who were not heavy drinkers. The subjects all drank an alcoholic cocktail and were given injections of a radioactive drug that binds to the brain's opioid receptors, to which natural painkillers known as endorphins bind. After analyzing the brains of all participants with positron-emission tomography imaging, the researchers could see that drinking alcohol released a flood of endorphins in two

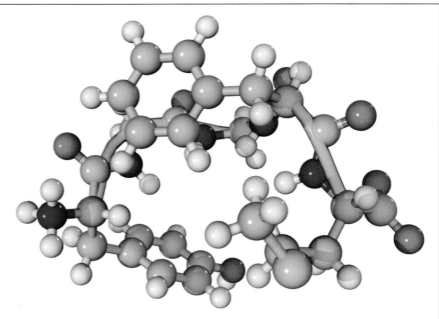

This computer generated image depicts a molecule of met-enkephalin, one of several natural pain-killing chemicals in the body known as endorphins. Drinking alcohol releases endorphins in the brain, which explains why it gives people feelings of pleasure.

specific brain areas: the nucleus accumbens, which is linked to reward-seeking behaviors and addiction; and the orbitofrontal cortex, which is involved in decision making. "This is something that we've speculated about for 30 years, based on animal studies, but haven't observed in humans until now," says Jennifer Mitchell, the center's clinical project director and lead study author. "It provides the first direct evidence of how alcohol makes people feel good."[46]

The study found that the more endorphins released in the nucleus accumbens, the greater the feelings of pleasure reported by each study participant. The more endorphins released in the orbitofrontal cortex, the greater the feelings of intoxication reported by the heavy drinkers, but not in members

> "Problem drinking has multiple causes, with genetic, physiological, psychological and social factors all playing a role."[48]
>
> —American Psychological Association, America's largest scientific and professional organization representing psychologists.

of the control group. "This indicates that the brains of heavy or problem drinkers are changed in a way that makes them more likely to find alcohol pleasant," says Mitchell, "and may be a clue to how problem drinking develops in the first place. That greater feeling of reward might cause them to drink too much."[47]

Family Ties

When people realize that they are alcoholics, it is common for them to agonize over why this happened, and why it is not possible for them to drink like "normal" people. They wonder what makes their brain different from the brains of people who do not develop drinking problems. Many question whether the problem is rooted in their childhood, their genes, the people with whom they associate, or their environment. The fact is, each person is unique, and some or even all of these factors may play a role in someone's development of alcoholism. "Problem drinking has multiple causes," says the American Psychological Association, "with genetic, physiological, psychological and social factors all playing a role."[48]

Even after decades of study, scientists have not yet identified a specific gene that is associated with alcoholism. They strongly suspect the culprit is not a single gene at all but rather a number of different ones. According to the NIAAA, the children of alcoholics are about four times more likely than the general population to develop alcohol problems. Erica, the young designer from Los Angeles, has a strong family history of drinking problems. "I come from a family of alcoholics," she says. "I watched how it affected my family life. But I never thought I would find myself here."[49]

Genetics is only part of a very complex picture, however, because genes alone cannot explain alcoholism. Most people with a family history of the disease do not go on to become alcoholics. What genes do is increase someone's vulnerability to developing alcohol problems. "Just because alcoholism tends to run in families," says the NIAAA, "does not mean that a child of an alcoholic parent will automatically become an alcoholic too. The risk is higher but it does not have to happen." That is where environmental factors come into play, as the NIAAA explains: "Genes are not the only things children inherit from their parents. How parents act and how they treat each other and their children has an influence on children growing up in the family. These aspects of family life also affect the risk for alcoholism."[50] When one or both parents drink heavily, and/or when there is frequent turmoil in the home environment, these factors can combine with genes to pave the way toward alcoholism. People who are troubled may drink in an effort to cope with their emotional problems, which psychologists refer to as *self-medicating*.

Mental Health Disorders and Alcoholism

There is also a strong association between alcoholism and mental health conditions such as anxiety, depression, schizophrenia, and bipolar disorder. According to SAMHSA, individuals with an alcohol use disorder are up to three times more likely to suffer from some type of anxiety disorder and are nearly four times more likely to suffer from major depression. Research has shown that depression is the most common mental health disorder in people with alcoholism. According to Shelly Greenfield, a professor of psychiatry at Harvard Medical School, about a third of people

A Fascinating Finding

In June 2015, researchers from the University of Vermont announced the results of a groundbreaking study related to alcoholism and genetics. They found that people with lighter eye color have a higher risk of becoming alcoholics than people with dark eyes.

For ten years Dawei Li, coauthor of the study, worked with scientists and physicians to build a clinical and genetic database of more than ten thousand people, most of whom are black or European Americans. Everyone in the database has, at some point, been addicted to alcohol or drugs. Using the database, Li and his team filtered out the alcohol-dependent patients of European ancestry, which totaled more than twelve hundred people. Arranging and rearranging various groups to compare participants' gender, age, and differences in ethnic backgrounds and geographic locations led the team to conclude that European Americans with light-colored eyes, especially blue eyes, had a higher rate of alcohol dependence than those with dark brown eyes. Another finding was that the genetic components that determine eye color line up along the same chromosomes as genes related to excessive alcohol use.

As intriguing as the study's findings were, it did not prove causation; researchers were unable to show a definitive link between eye color and alcoholism risk. Still, the study paved the way for additional exploration of the relationship between alcoholism and genetic traits such as eye color. "There is a lot to be untangled here," says study coauthor Arvis Sulovari, "and we may have only uncovered the tip of the iceberg."

Quoted in April Burbank, "UVM Eye-Color Study Goes Viral," *Burlington Free Press*, July 2, 2015. www .burlingtonfreepress.com.

who are depressed also have a problem with alcohol. Usually, but not always, the depression comes first.

The connection between depression and alcoholism is so strong and so common that alcoholism is sometimes believed to be a form of depression, although this is not correct. PsychCentral associate editor Therese J. Borchard, who has been recovered from alcoholism for more than twenty-five years, refers to this mistaken belief as "the chicken-egg thing." She writes, "People get depressed after ingesting a depressant liquid like whiskey. And people drink to self-medicate the pain of depression. When the initial buzz wears off, they need even more of the whiskey to achieve the same result, causing even more depression. And so the vicious cycle begins."[51]

Childhood Trauma and Alcoholism

It is well known among addiction specialists that childhood trauma such as physical, emotional, and/or sexual abuse vastly increases the chances that someone will develop alcohol problems later in life. Studies have clearly shown that children who suffer from abuse and/or neglect develop substance abuse problems as adults at far higher rates than adults with no history of childhood trauma. "Trauma is particularly damaging when it occurs in childhood," says addiction psychiatrist David Sack. "Young children do not have a frame of reference to put traumatic experiences in context or try to make sense of them. Their primary outlet for support is the family, which is often the source of trauma in cases of abuse or neglect." As these children grow older, they may turn to substances as a way to cope with unresolved emotional pain. "Rather than thinking about or reliving the event," says Sack, "the individual may use drugs, alcohol, or other substances or behaviors to numb feelings of fear, powerlessness or depression or to cope with intrusive memories."[52]

A 2013 study conducted by a team of NIAAA researchers focused on examining the association between childhood trauma and alcoholism in adults. The study involved more than four hundred people, of whom 280 had sought treatment for alcoholism. The remainder had no history of alcohol dependence and made up the control group. All participants were assessed for a history of childhood trauma, including physical abuse, physical neglect, sexual abuse, emotional neglect, and emotional abuse. Of those who had experienced childhood trauma, the researchers evaluated how severe the trauma had been.

The study revealed that childhood trauma was significantly more prevalent among the people who sought treatment for alcoholism as adults. Moreover, the severity of their drinking problem

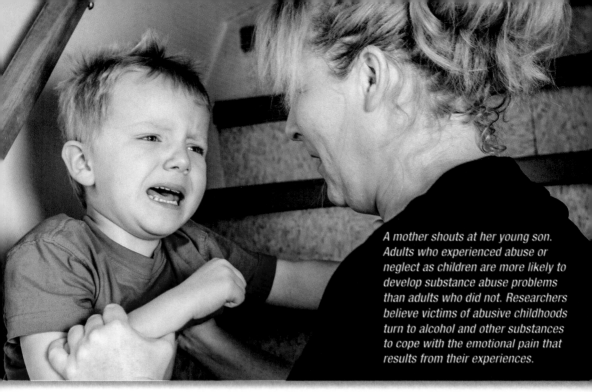

A mother shouts at her young son. Adults who experienced abuse or neglect as children are more likely to develop substance abuse problems than adults who did not. Researchers believe victims of abusive childhoods turn to alcohol and other substances to cope with the emotional pain that results from their experiences.

was closely aligned with how severe their childhood trauma had been. "In other words," says clinical psychologist Joseph Nowinski, "the greater the childhood abuse or neglect, the more severe the adult drinking problem would be." Nowinski says that the study findings are important for two reasons: "First, they support the notion that genetics alone are not sufficient to account for a person's vulnerability to addiction. In a word, *experience* matters. Second, they point a direction for areas that need to be explored in treatment."[53]

More Questions than Answers

Even after many years of research, alcoholism remains shrouded in mystery. Scientists widely agree that it is a condition rooted in brain chemistry—a condition that involves strong cravings for alcohol, the inability to control drinking, dependence on alcohol, and a physical tolerance that leads to heavier and heavier drinking. Although decades of study has revealed a number of contributing factors for alcoholism, there is still a great deal that remains unknown.

CHAPTER 4: Treatment and Recovery Challenges

L ucy Rocca knew she had a serious alcohol problem, but it took a brush with death for her to actually give up drinking. Even then it was not an easy decision, however. Drinking was an integral part of her life; it was how she relaxed and unwound at home and had fun socializing with her friends. She saw this all around her, observing that in Britain (where she lives) "the predominant message is that alcohol is a prerequisite for letting your hair down and living it up." Rocca herself shared that belief. After drinking for twenty years, having fun without alcohol was inconceivable. "Drinking defined me," she says. "I adored its recklessness and its glamour. I loved the confidence it sprinkled liberally over my personality." She viewed nondrinkers as "either boring or do-gooders"[54] and was convinced that without drinking life would be boring—and so would she. That viewpoint changed in April 2011, when Rocca was so badly frightened that she gave up alcohol for good.

The Turning Point

Alone at home one evening, Rocca drank glass after glass of wine until she had finished a bottle. She opened another and polished off that as well. Although she has no memory of it, she finished a third bottle of wine too. At some point she stumbled outside and collapsed unconscious on the pavement. Fortunately for Rocca an acquaintance driving by spotted her and called an ambulance. She woke up in the middle of the night in a hospital with glaring lights in her eyes and no idea whatsoever how she had gotten there or what had happened. That, for Rocca, was what many alcoholics refer to as their rock bottom. "I finally accepted in that hospital bed that I would never be able to control how much I drank," says Rocca, "and that if I continued to drink alcohol, I would die prematurely leaving my daughter motherless. I never drank again."[55]

Once Rocca made up her mind to stop drinking, she developed her own treatment plan. Although she drank regularly for two decades, she had not developed a physical dependence on alcohol. Thus, she did not need a detoxification or formal rehab program. She committed herself to a sober life and read numerous books about alcohol dependence. She went to a therapist for help unraveling the reasons why she drank so much for so long. She became interested in a healthier lifestyle and began running as well as practicing meditation. Yet as motivated as Rocca was, this was not an easy time for her. "My life stretched out in front of me like a tiresome, repetitive treadmill of work and sleep," she says, "with no more injections of fun and hedonism to brighten things up."[56]

It took more than a year, but Rocca finally began to see that she was making progress rebuilding a life that did not revolve around drinking. Formerly uneasy with people she did not know, she now found that she could interact with them without feeling self-conscious. There were other changes as well. "I gradually came to acknowledge the unthinkable—I actually liked being a non-drinker," she says. "I was different without alcohol. I wasn't a bad person who hated her own reflection and woke in the middle of the night being eaten alive by regrets and shame. I felt as though I'd discovered a magic solution to all that had been wrong with my life, and it was so simple: just don't drink alcohol."[57]

> "I gradually came to acknowledge the unthinkable—I actually liked being a non-drinker. I was different without alcohol."[57]
>
> —Lucy Rocca, a woman from the United Kingdom who recovered from alcoholism.

Fundamental Steps Toward Sobriety

For many people, though, quitting drinking is extraordinarily difficult. Because of the risks involved, these people should not try to get sober on their own. Rather, they need a medically supervised detox program, followed by treatment for alcoholism. Without medical supervision, someone who has been dependent on alcohol for a long time is at risk of serious, and possibly life-threatening, complications. "Anyone with a serious dependency on alcohol should never even consider going 'cold turkey' at home. . . . When a person stops drinking alcohol suddenly, just up and quits because he or she thinks it's time to do so and it's easy to do, the consequences can be deadly," says the substance abuse treatment program Elements Behavioral Health. "Sudden alcohol cessation can cause hallucinations, convulsions, and even heart seizure that may result in death. This isn't something to take lightly and is an excellent reason not to try to detox from alcohol at home."[58]

Detox is sometimes called the cleansing process because its purpose is to cleanse the body of all traces of alcohol, which usually takes about a week. During detox, patients may experience a wide range of symptoms associated with alcohol withdrawal, such as headaches, nausea, drenching sweat, and chills. This

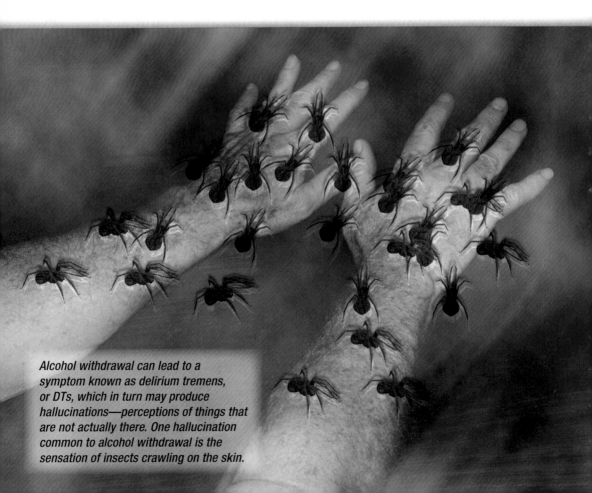

Alcohol withdrawal can lead to a symptom known as delirium tremens, or DTs, which in turn may produce hallucinations—perceptions of things that are not actually there. One hallucination common to alcohol withdrawal is the sensation of insects crawling on the skin.

is because in the same way that drinking alters brain chemistry, depriving the brain of alcohol does as well. "When heavy drinkers suddenly stop or significantly reduce their alcohol consumption, the neurotransmitters previously suppressed by alcohol are no longer suppressed," explains physician Jennifer Robinson. "They rebound, resulting in a phenomenon known as brain hyperexcitability. So, the effects associated with alcohol withdrawal— anxiety, irritability, agitation, tremors, seizures, and DTs [delirium tremens]— are the opposite of those associated with alcohol consumption."[59]

DTs are the most severe and dangerous risk of alcohol withdrawal, and people suffering from the condition must be closely monitored. According to psychiatric nurse Rita K. Driver, DTs are fatal in up to 20 percent of patients who do not receive medical attention. An individual experiencing DTs may suffer from fever, agitation, hallucinations (seeing or hearing things that are not there), extreme confusion, and seizures. Because of the severe risks involved, DTs must be treated in a hospital setting, with close monitoring of vital signs and blood chemistry, and possibly with medication to keep the patient calm and relaxed. Once someone has finished the detox phase, his or her body has been cleansed of alcohol, but that is only the beginning of the journey to sobriety. "Detox rids the body of poison," says the chemical dependency program Promises Treatment Centers, "but does nothing to address the healing and re-education which is needed to take place before an addiction can be overcome."[60]

> "When a person stops drinking alcohol suddenly, just up and quits because he or she thinks it's time to do so and it's easy to do, the consequences can be deadly."[58]
>
> —Elements Behavioral Health, a substance abuse treatment program headquartered in Long Beach, California.

Treatment Options

The "healing and re-education," which refers to comprehensive alcoholism treatment, is indeed essential for someone to recover from alcoholism—but according to the NIAAA, only a small fraction of the millions of people who need treatment actually receive it.

There are numerous reasons for this, with the biggest hurdle being cost. Alcohol rehab programs can be extraordinarily expensive, with the most posh facilities costing upwards of $1,800 per day—an amount that is out of reach for all but the wealthiest patients.

The various reasons alcoholics do not get the treatment they need were discussed in a May 2015 investigative story in *Mother Jones* magazine. The story emphasized the cost barrier, stating that the number-one reason people are not treated for addiction to alcohol or other drugs is that they cannot afford treatment and/or have inadequate health coverage. Nearly one-quarter of people who need treatment do not seek it because they are not ready to quit drinking or using drugs. The remainder either do not know where to go for treatment, lack transportation to get there, or are worried that pursuing treatment might jeopardize their jobs.

For those who do seek treatment, choosing a recovery program can seem overwhelming. "The important thing," says Promises Treatment Centers, "is that rehab will address the various ways that alcohol has become an addiction and the residual effects of the abuse."[61] Treatment programs are loosely grouped into two categories: inpatient residential, in which patients live onsite during the entire treatment process, and outpatient, whereby patients travel to the facility for treatment but live independently.

According to Joseph Goldberg, who is a clinical professor of psychiatry at the Icahn School of Medicine at Mount Sinai Hospital in New York City, residential programs can last from a month to more than a year. They are so named because they take place in a residential environment, meaning a homelike setting. The patient's treatment is often divided into a series of stages. "In the beginning, a patient's contact with others, including friends and family, is strictly limited," explains Goldberg. "The idea is to develop a primary relationship with the other residents who are also recovering from alcoholism. Eventually, the person will be allowed more contact with people outside the residential community and may even go back to work or school, returning home to the treatment facility each day."[62]

Outpatient programs are offered at hospitals, health clinics, community mental health clinics, counselors' offices, and residential facilities that have outpatient clinics. Goldberg says that attendance requirements vary, and many of these programs are

Most Alcoholics Do Not Seek Help

Research has shown that tens of millions of people in the United States suffer from some level of alcohol use disorder, yet a minority of them seek treatment.

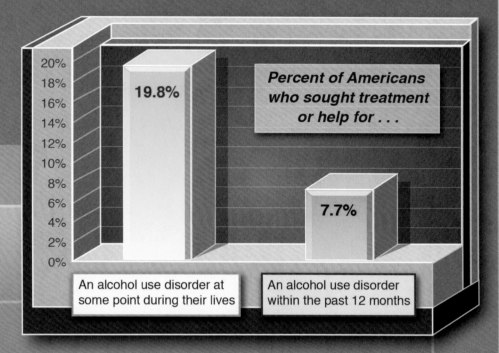

Percent of Americans who sought treatment or help for . . .

19.8% — An alcohol use disorder at some point during their lives

7.7% — An alcohol use disorder within the past 12 months

Source: JAMA Network, "Alcohol Use Disorder Is Widespread, Often Untreated in the United States," June 3, 2015. http://media.jamanetwork.com.

run in the evenings and on weekends so patients can continue working while they participate in treatment. More intensive outpatient programs require nine to twenty hours of treatment per week and run for two months to one year. These, according to Goldberg, "work best for people who are motivated to participate and who have supportive families and friends."[63]

It is widely believed that alcoholics have an extremely high relapse rate. Addiction experts stress, however, that determining the exact number of alcoholics who relapse is difficult and challenging. There are few studies that have focused on relapse rates, although one eight-year study published in 2007 is described by psychiatrist Omar Manejwala as "the most thorough attempt to understand what happens to addicts and alcoholics who stay sober." The researchers followed nearly twelve hundred addicts and alcoholics and found that "extended abstinence really does predict long term recovery."[64] Manejwala says there were three key findings: Only about a third of people who are abstinent less than a year will remain abstinent. For those who achieve a year of sobriety, fewer than half will relapse. Finally, if someone can make it to five years of sobriety, his or her chance of relapse drops to less than 15 percent.

Looking Within

For people who give up alcohol after years of heavy drinking, the emotional aspects of their newfound sobriety can be extremely difficult. It is common for alcoholics to turn to alcohol in an effort to mask their trauma, stress, or depression. Alcohol becomes their escape—without it, they must face disturbing feelings and problems, and this can seem unbearable. A psychologist or other trained therapist can help people overcome those negative feelings and learn how to address their emotional problems without trying to drink them away. Therapy, says the American Psychological Association, "can help people boost their motivation to stop drinking, identify circumstances that trigger drinking, learn new methods to cope with high-risk drinking situations, and develop social support systems within their own communities."[65]

There are many types of therapy that alcoholism counselors can recommend based on their patients' individual needs. One type is cognitive behavioral therapy, which seeks to change negative, destructive thoughts to positive, healthy ones. Patients learn to identify feelings and situations (called *cues*) that have led to heavy alcohol use and to develop the skills necessary to cope with problems that might trigger drinking. Another method, motivational enhancement therapy, can help patients build and strengthen motivation to change drinking behavior. This type of therapy, according to the NIAAA, helps patients develop a plan for making changes in their lives as well as on building confidence and developing the skills they need to stick to the plan.

Elizabeth Vargas, who is an anchor for ABC News, spent more than a month in an alcoholism rehab program, and therapy played a major role in her recovery. For years she had suffered from anxiety and panic attacks and began using alcohol as a way to cope with her feelings. "I dealt with that anxiety, and with the stress that the anxiety brought by starting to drink," says Vargas. "And it slowly escalated and got worse and worse." Through the intensive therapy she underwent during her time in rehab, she learned to recognize the stressors that triggered her drinking. She also learned that alcohol was not the right way to handle stress. "Listen, there are lots of people who feel a lot of stress," says Vargas. "Not everybody turns to a glass of wine or three like I did, or four, like I did on some occasions." Through therapy, she learned that rather than masking her feelings with alcohol, she needed to feel them. "You know what?," says Vargas. "They're not going to kill you. You have to experience them. I never learned that skill and (it) makes it tough some days. Alcohol for me is no longer an option."[66]

> "Listen, there are lots of people who feel a lot of stress. Not everybody turns to a glass of wine or three like I did, or four, like I did on some occasions."[66]
>
> —Elizabeth Vargas, an anchorwoman for ABC News who recovered from alcoholism.

The Twelve-Step Approach

Once Vargas finished the rehab program, she joined AA and regularly attends meetings. She says that being a member of AA has been a rewarding experience. "I have a sponsor. I have great, great friends who I love and who love me."[67] Millions of people throughout the world share Vargas's affection for AA, saying that it helped them get sober and stay that way. It is based on the twelve-step approach, in which members read and study a manual known as the *Big Book of Alcoholics Anonymous* and work their way through a set of steps that serve as instructions for achieving sobriety and living a sober life.

AA is famous throughout the world and is the most widely accepted of all programs for people who seek help for alcoholism—but not everyone believes that to be positive. Because it is a fellowship (an association of like-minded individuals) rather than an accredited treatment program, AA is often criticized for not being based on science. Another common criticism is AA's premise that alcoholism is a progressive disease that can never be cured; therefore, an alcoholic's only chance at becoming sober is to admit powerlessness over alcohol, turn to a higher power for help,

The Twelve Steps

Alcoholics Anonymous (AA) was founded in the 1930s and is the most widely known approach to helping people with alcoholism. Although not everyone subscribes to the AA philosophy, and it has its share of detractors, millions of people throughout the world are convinced it is the key to sobriety. The program is based on a dozen principles that are known as the Twelve Steps:

1. We admitted we were powerless over alcohol—that our lives had become unmanageable.
2. Came to believe that a Power greater than ourselves could restore us to sanity.
3. Made a decision to turn our will and our lives over to the care of God *as we understood Him.*
4. Made a searching and fearless moral inventory of ourselves.
5. Admitted to God, to ourselves, and to another human being the exact nature of our wrongs.
6. Were entirely ready to have God remove all these defects of character.
7. Humbly asked Him to remove our shortcomings.
8. Made a list of all persons we had harmed, and became willing to make amends to them all.
9. Made direct amends to such people wherever possible, except when to do so would injure them or others.
10. Continued to take personal inventory and when we were wrong promptly admitted it.
11. Sought through prayer and meditation to improve our conscious contact with God, *as we understood Him*, praying only for knowledge of His will for us and the power to carry that out.
12. Having had a spiritual awakening as the result of these Steps, we tried to carry this message to alcoholics, and to practice these principles in all our affairs.

Silkworth, "The Twelve Steps of Alcoholics Anonymous," 2015. http://silkworth.net.

and attend AA meetings indefinitely. This premise, according to AA critics, is deeply flawed. One of the program's harshest critics is Lance Dodes, a retired Harvard Medical School professor of psychiatry. "Twelve steps sounds like science; it feels like rigor; it has the syntax of a roadmap," says Dodes. "Yet when we examine these twelve steps more closely, we find dubious ideas and even some potentially harmful myths."[68]

Lee Ann Kaskutas, a senior scientist at the Alcohol Research Group, disagrees with Dodes's negative opinion of AA. She says that one of the most valuable attributes of the program is that people battling alcoholism develop a strong social network with others who are going through the same thing, and this can be a powerful motivator to not drink. Kaskutas says that critics who tend to focus on AA's quirks or spiritual aspect are missing the point of why it works well for so many people. "When you think about a mechanism like supportive social networks, or the psychological benefit of helping others," she says, "well, they have nothing to do with faith, or God—they have to do with the reality

Plagued by PAWS

When alcoholics are able to quit drinking, they typically feel elated. Getting sober is a major accomplishment, one that takes hard work and dedication; those who achieve it are understandably proud of themselves. They anticipate that without the burden of alcohol, their health will improve and they will start to feel better than they have in years.

Therefore, many are confused and distraught when, two or three months after their last drink, they are suddenly plagued by fatigue, mood swings, memory loss, and insomnia. They wonder why they feel worse instead of better. It is likely that no one warned them about post-acute withdrawal syndrome (PAWS), which by definition is delayed withdrawal symptoms. Scientists suspect that PAWS is the result of the brain trying to regain homeostasis, meaning its normal balanced state. "The brain has tremendous capacity to heal," says addiction psychiatrist David Sack, "but it doesn't heal quickly."

How long PAWS lasts or how severe it is depends on the individual. In most cases, symptoms last no longer than a month, but there have been reports of the syndrome lingering much longer. Sack emphasizes that alcohol has long-term physical consequences because of how it changes brain chemistry. There is a "whole host of wiring that actually gets worse" four to eight weeks after someone has quit drinking. Unfortunately, says Sack, people often experience these symptoms about the time they are released from rehab. "We're sending people out when this is getting worse."

Quoted in Jeanene Swanson, "The Condition That Many Recovering Addicts and Alcoholics Don't Know About," Huffington Post, February 12, 2014. www.huffingtonpost.com.

of what goes on in AA, with people meeting others in the same boat as they are in, and with helping other people."[69]

Medication-Assisted Treatment

Of the various approaches for treating people with alcoholism, medication-assisted treatment has proven effective in helping people stop or reduce their drinking as well as to avoid relapse. Those who frown on the method often have the impression that taking medication is just trading one addiction for another, but this is not true. "All medications approved for treating alcohol dependence are non-addictive," says the NIAAA. "These medicines are designed to help manage a chronic disease, just as someone might take drugs to keep their asthma or diabetes in check."[70]

The three medications the Food and Drug Administration has approved for treating alcohol dependence include Naltrexone, which helps the patient reduce heavy drinking; Acamprosate, which makes it easier to maintain abstinence; and Disulfiram, which interferes with the body's ability to metabolize alcohol. This results in unpleasant symptoms such as nausea and flushed skin, which can dissuade patients from drinking while taking the drug.

After numerous unsuccessful attempts to quit drinking, actress Claudia Christian finally achieved sobriety by using Naltrexone. "I went to dozens of Alcoholics Anonymous meetings in two different countries," she says. "I tried moderation. I tried tapering. I tried hypnosis. I tried rehab. I tried everything." Then, in 2009, as Christian was leaving a detox facility in California, she noticed a flyer for Vivitrol, an injectable form of Naltrexone. She learned that the drug is designed to block endorphins from reaching their targeted receptors in the brain. Her doctor prescribed the drug, Christian started taking it, and finally she was able to recover from alcoholism. Today she is an outspoken advocate of the drug and spends time and resources educating others about it. "I wish someone had done it for me when I was searching for an answer to my alcohol problem,"[71] she says.

> "I went to dozens of Alcoholics Anonymous meetings in two different countries. I tried moderation. I tried tapering. I tried hypnosis. I tried rehab. I tried everything."[71]
>
> —Claudia Christian, an actress who recovered from alcoholism by taking the drug Naltrexone.

Recovery Is Possible

Alcoholism is a tough, challenging condition to overcome. Many different options are available, from rehab programs and AA to medication-assisted treatment. Unfortunately, however, most people do not get the treatment they need, and even those who do have a high chance of relapsing. As scientists continue to explore alcoholism-related research, better treatment methods will hopefully become available.

CHAPTER 5: How Can Alcohol Abuse Be Prevented?

It is the prevailing belief among addiction experts that the key to preventing alcoholism in adults is to reach out to young people. "Addiction is a pediatric disease," says John Knight, the founder and director of the Center for Adolescent Substance Abuse Research at Boston Children's Hospital. "When adults entering addiction treatment are asked when they first began drinking or using drugs, the answer is almost always the same: They started when they were young—teenagers."[72]

Knight emphasizes how profoundly drug and/or alcohol use can affect the adolescent brain. Not only are young people more likely to make bad choices than adults, but they are also much more vulnerable to becoming addicted. "When people start using at a younger age, the changes in brain structure and function are very, very pronounced," he says. "If we could only get kids to postpone their first drink or their first use of drugs, we could greatly diminish the prevalence of addiction in the U.S." In an effort to achieve that, public health officials, physicians, and addiction specialists are emphasizing the importance of prevention programs targeted at youth. "If we don't prevent it during the teen years," says Knight, "we're really missing the boat."[73]

"If we could only get kids to postpone their first drink or their first use of drugs, we could greatly diminish the prevalence of addiction in the U.S."[73]

—John Knight, the founder and director of the Center for Adolescent Substance Abuse Research at Boston Children's Hospital.

Catching Trouble Early

One of the leading prevention strategies is the Screening, Brief Intervention, and Referral to Treatment (SBIRT) program. Designed to prevent and/or treat substance abuse at an early age, the SBIRT method has been implemented in schools and afterschool programs throughout the United States. It is also used at primary health care centers, hospital emergency rooms, trauma centers, and other health care facilities.

The screening portion of the program involves pediatricians, who now routinely screen young patients for substance problems during their annual visits. This is a major change from a few decades ago, and according to Sharon Levy, a physician who directs the adolescent substance abuse program at Boston Children's Hospital, a welcome one. "I interpret that as a real shift in culture," says Levy, "from one in which there was controversy over whether drug use was a legitimate topic for pediatricians to address to one in which it's now part of the standard of care." She views the pediatrician's office as an ideal place to discuss substance abuse with patients, calling it a "unique setting in which an adolescent gets to have a confidential conversation"[74] with a trusted adult who is not a parent.

As part of a program that has been implemented at schools and health care facilities across the country, doctors are encouraged to screen teen patients for substance abuse problems during routine visits. Here, a doctor consults with a teen boy.

If troubling behavior is uncovered during screening, a brief intervention takes place. That might be nothing more than a conversation between the doctor and patient that includes "science and stories," two elements that Knight says are crucial for getting the prevention message across to young people. He explains: "What they want from doctors is, 'Tell us what the science is, don't tell us what to do; give us the information and trust us to make the right decisions.'"[75]

In lieu of a doctor, the person who conducts the brief intervention could be a therapist or counselor, such as Elizabeth D'Amico, a

Five-Star States

Since 2006, Mothers Against Drunk Driving (MADD) has issued an annual report that rates US states' efforts to prevent drunk driving. To determine the ratings, MADD looks at five different action steps, called countermeasures, and awards states one star for each step that has been implemented. One countermeasure is the presence of ignition interlock laws, which pertain to devices installed in cars of past offenders that measure blood alcohol level. Another is whether the state conducts sobriety checkpoints, which are random stops by law enforcement that screen drivers for intoxication. "While all countermeasures are important to improve a state's drunk driving laws," says MADD, "we know that ignition interlocks and sobriety checkpoints are the two most effective ways to dramatically reduce fatalities and injuries."

The remaining three countermeasures are license revocation laws (which allow an officer to seize the driver's license of someone stopped for drunk driving); child endangerment laws (which consider driving under the influence with a child in the vehicle as a form of child abuse); and no-refusal laws (laws that allow officers to quickly and easily obtain a warrant to conduct Breathalyzer or blood tests).

The January 2015 MADD report shows that thirteen states had all countermeasures in place and received a five-star rating: Alabama, Arizona, Colorado, Delaware, Illinois, Kansas, Maine, Mississippi, Missouri, Nebraska, Utah, Virginia, and West Virginia.

Mothers Against Drunk Driving, "2015 Report to the Nation," January 2015. www.madd.org.

clinical psychologist and senior behavioral scientist at the research and policy organization Rand Corporation. D'Amico developed a voluntary afterschool prevention and intervention program for middle school youth called Choice. The program is so named because, according to D'Amico, voluntary programs appeal more to youth because they can choose to attend rather than being forced to do so. At the heart of her program is a technique called motivational interviewing, which she uses during interventions with young people. She says it is about "guiding someone to make a healthy choice, versus saying, 'Okay, you have a problem and you need to change.'" D'Amico adds that anyone who works with youth needs to acknowledge that there are reasons why young people use alcohol or drugs.

> "You lose all your credibility if you just say, 'It's bad for you, stop.'"[76]
>
> —Elizabeth D'Amico, a clinical psychologist and senior behavioral scientist at the research and policy organization Rand Corporation.

"You lose all your credibility if you just say, 'It's bad for you, stop.'"[76] D'Amico explains that motivational interviewing is more collaborative than merely telling a teen what to do. For example, if teens admit that they drink to relax, the counselor can help them explore other, healthier ways of relieving stress.

Kids Educating Kids

Prevention programs such as Choice represent one strategy for educating kids about substance abuse. There are innumerable other programs in place throughout the United States as well. One is in Gwinnett County, Georgia, where county health officials have seen the prevalence of drinking among high school students steadily decline since 2008. In addition, the current prevalence is lower than the national average; a youth health survey conducted during 2014 in Gwinnett County found that 19 percent of high school students had used alcohol during the past month, compared with 22.6 percent as shown in the 2014 Monitoring the Future survey of high school risk behaviors.

Gwinnett County health officials attribute this positive trend to several programs that try to prevent teen substance abuse. One is the Youth Advisory Board (YAB), in which high school students serve as mentors and leaders to their fellow students. Supported by staff members, the teen leaders attend monthly meetings, participate in community-wide events, and attend a summer leadership program called the Georgia Teen Institute. Here, YAB leaders learn leadership skills and plan their prevention initiatives for the school year. These include prevention campaigns with titles such as Save Brains, Safe and Sober Prom, and Parents Who Host Lose the Most, among others.

One event, held during the fall of 2015, featured an obstacle course race for youth and adults. Designed to illustrate the effects of alcohol on someone's behavior, the event took place with some people wearing goggles, which put them at a disadvantage against those who were not wearing goggles. Other YAB activities include planning and implementing community events, public speaking, and networking opportunities. One YAB student leader, Naja Nelson, says she has gained a wealth of experience by being involved in the program. Before becoming a YAB leader, she knew that alcohol and drugs were bad, but she is now clearly aware of the risks; moreover, she can pass factual information along to other students. "Because of the knowledge gained," says Nelson, "I am able to share it with my friends, help them rationalize and not excuse their behavior. I had to have a conversation with my friend this week about a particular Snapchat she posted and how it's not okay."[77]

The Shock Factor

Educating teens about the dangers of drinking and driving is among the highest priorities for law enforcement and traffic safety officials. Many are convinced that shock can be an effective deterrent and thus have developed prevention programs that are designed to shock young people into facing the dire results of mixing alcohol with driving. One such program is called Every 15 Minutes. The title is based on a statistic showing how often people in the United States have died due to drunk driving.

On the first day, a person who is dressed as the Grim Reaper visits a classroom every fifteen minutes and quickly whisks a student away. At the student's empty desk, a volunteer places a

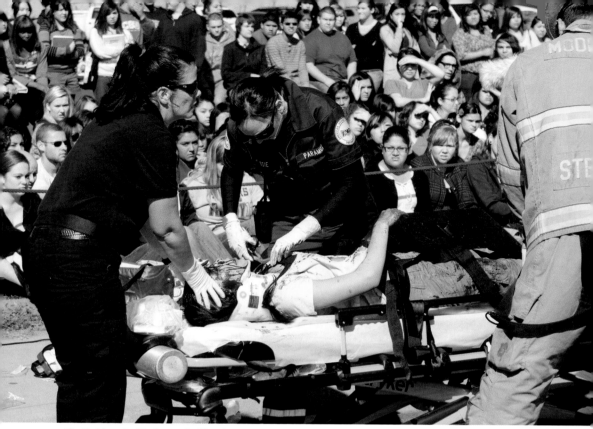

Firefighters in Modesto, California, tend to the victim of a simulated drunk-driving crash as part of an "Every 15 Minutes" event. The program, whose name derives from statistics showing how frequently people in the United States die as the result of drunk driving, is intended to shock young people into confronting the grim results of driving while intoxicated.

memorial: a sash bearing the student's name and a black rose. A police officer immediately enters the classroom and reads an obituary written by the "dead" student's parents, explaining the circumstances of his or her death and how it has devastated their family. A few minutes later the student, wearing white face makeup, a coroner's tag, and a black "Every 15 Minutes" T-shirt, returns to the class but does not speak or interact with other students for the remainder of the school day. He or she has now become one of the living dead. In the afternoon, a simulated traffic crash takes place on the school grounds, with graphically realistic injuries, deaths, and drunk-driving arrests.

In April 2015 students at San Benito High School in Hollister, California, attended an Every 15 Minutes presentation—and like most others who have seen one, they were left shaken by the

Prohibition: A Failed Policy

Some experts advocate tougher laws as a strategy for preventing alcohol abuse. Those who are opposed maintain there are already enough laws in place, and it is not up to the government to regulate people's behavior. A common argument against more government regulation is the failure of Prohibition, which began on January 19, 1920, when Congress ratified the Eighteenth Amendment. Prohibition banned the manufacture and distribution of alcoholic beverages, with the goal of reducing alcohol consumption and decreasing crime.

The reality, however, was quite the opposite. Once alcohol became illegal, demand for it soared, which led to the growth of organized crime. Companies that could no longer legally make and distribute alcoholic beverages went out of business. They were replaced by mobsters who were eager to make millions of dollars on the black market. Street gangs formed, crime escalated, and the prison population exploded. According to economist Mark Thornton, while violent crime had been declining in the years prior to Prohibition, the homicide rate increased 78 percent during the 1920s. Prohibition also became a major contributor to corruption, as Thornton explains: "Everyone from major politicians to the cop on the beat took bribes from bootleggers, moonshiners, crime bosses, and owners of speakeasies."

In 1933 Congress acknowledged that Prohibition had been a miserable failure and took steps to repeal the Eighteenth Amendment. Almost immediately, crime began to drop and continued to decline over the following years.

Mark Thornton, "Alcohol Prohibition Was a Failure," Cato Institute Policy Analysis No. 157, July 17, 1991. www.cato.org.

experience. On the second day of the program they attended a mock funeral for the victims and watched a video of the prior day's events. Many students had to keep reminding themselves that it was not real because they were so deeply affected by it. This was true of Riley Lange, a senior varsity baseball player who was one of the living dead. He called the experience "life-changing" and said it gave him a "whole new perspective on life." He now realizes how crucial it is to never drink and drive. "When something like that happens, it doesn't just affect you, it affects the whole community," says Lange, "and it's not just a short-term thing, it's a lifelong thing, that you'd have to live with every day."[78]

Strategies for Colleges

Prevention programs are widespread at high schools throughout the United States; the same is not true of colleges, however. Because of the alarming prevalence of binge drinking by college students, the need for implementing prevention programs is especially great. According to David Rosenbloom, a professor at Boston University's School of Public Health, there is a dearth of prevention programs at colleges and universities despite evidence of the need for them. "There is a striking disconnect between the research that demonstrates effective population and individual ways to prevent and reduce harm and the reality of what happens on most campuses," Rosenbloom explained in a May 2015 report on the issue. "Very few colleges have implemented and sustained the kind of comprehensive campus/community strategies that research has shown can be effective in reducing and preventing alcohol related harms."[79]

Along with an in-depth discussion of the problem, Rosenbloom suggests a number of ways communities could curtail alcohol abuse. These include raising the price of alcohol through tax increases, placing bans on low-priced happy hours, and banning or limiting kegs and other high-quantity serving methods that are common at large college parties. "Low prices and easy availability of essentially unlimited amounts of alcohol, especially served in large containers in poorly supervised settings, create an almost insurmountable barrier to effective action to prevent and reduce,"[80] says Rosenbloom. More consistent enforcement of the legal drinking age is another recommendation, as is creating and promoting activities that do not revolve around excessive drinking. Rosenbloom also suggests that colleges schedule more classes on Fridays, which could potentially reduce the large number of students who binge drink on Thursday nights.

"Low prices and easy availability of essentially unlimited amounts of alcohol, especially served in large containers in poorly supervised settings, create an almost insurmountable barrier to effective action to prevent and reduce."[80]

—David Rosenbloom, a professor at Boston University's School of Public Health.

Another preventive measure involves using technology such as geotargeting. This refers to the practice of delivering content to someone based on his or her geographic location. Calling this "in-the-moment delivery," Rosenbloom says this could enable text messages to be sent to a student who has been identified as a high risk at the time and place where heavy drinking might be taking place. An August 2015 article about the issue explains, "Imagine heading out to a neighborhood bar and getting an automatic text reminder to moderate your drinking. Or logging the number of beers you consume into an app on your phone, which sends you personalized messages when you hit a predetermined limit."[81] Rosenbloom and other experts say that these preventive measures could go a long way toward helping colleges and universities curb prolific drinking among students.

The Drinking Age Debate

Of all the preventive measures that have been implemented over the years, none is more controversial than the drinking age. Until the early 1980s, it was up to individual states to establish the drinking age. Nearly all had designated twenty-one as the legal age after the end of Prohibition, the era from 1920 to 1933 when alcohol was illegal in the United States. In 1971, when the Twenty-Sixth Amendment to the US Constitution lowered the voting age to eighteen, two-thirds of the states correspondingly lowered their legal drinking age. Then, in 1984, Congress passed a law that gave states a financial incentive to raise the drinking age; they were not required to do so, but those who chose not to raise the drinking age risked losing some federal highway funding. As a result, every US state currently has a legal drinking age of twenty-one.

The drinking age has become a controversial issue, one that led to the founding of the Amethyst Initiative, an organization whose tagline is "Rethink the Drinking Age." The Amethyst Initiative is made up of chancellors and presidents of colleges and universities throughout the United States who collectively maintain that the drinking age of twenty-one is not an effective deterrent to drunk driving. One of the founders is John M. McCardell, the former president of Middlebury College. In May 2012

Americans Favor a Drinking Age of Twenty-One

The current legal drinking age in every US state is twenty-one. To prevent underage drinking and driving, most people strongly favor keeping it that way. This was one finding of a June 2015 Gallup poll, which revealed that nearly three-fourths of respondents opposed efforts to lower the drinking age nationwide to eighteen.

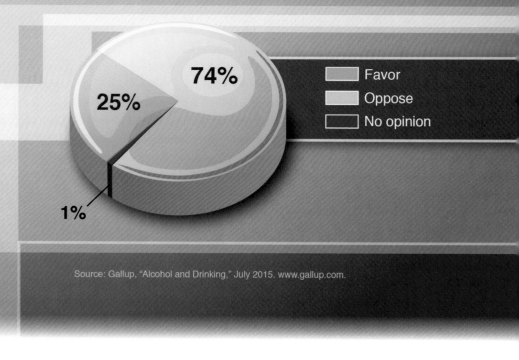

Would you favor or oppose a federal law that would lower the drinking age in all states to 18?

74%

25%

1%

☐ Favor
☐ Oppose
☐ No opinion

Source: Gallup, "Alcohol and Drinking," July 2015. www.gallup.com.

McCardell published a bold editorial in the *New York Times* in which he wrote, "Although our laws acknowledge that at age 18 young adults possess sufficient maturity and judgment to operate a motor vehicle, serve in the military, perform jury duty or sign a contract, those same laws deny 18-year-olds the right to purchase, possess or consume alcohol." In the same editorial, McCardell claimed an association between a lower drinking age and binge drinking among young people. "If you infantilize someone," he says, "do not be surprised when infantile behavior—like binge drinking—results. Prohibition is not the answer, and never has been."[82]

Health officials, law enforcement, and addiction experts widely disagree with McCardell and the other signatories to the Amethyst Initiative, however. According to William DeJong, a professor at Boston University's School of Public Health, there is an undeniable correlation between a higher drinking age and fewer deaths from alcohol-related crashes. DeJong, along with Boston University public health researcher Jason Blanchette, conducted an extensive review of research published since 2006. That year was chosen because it was when the organization Choose Responsibility called for the government to repeal the 1984 Minimum Drinking Age Act. The title of the published study is indicative of what the researchers found while conducting it: "Case Closed: Research Evidence on the Positive Public Health Impact of the Age 21 Minimum Legal Drinking Age in the United States." In the published study, DeJong and Blanchette emphasize the importance of keeping the legal drinking at twenty-one. "The current law has served the nation well,"[83] they write.

DeJong is convinced that, along with keeping a higher drinking age, education can help discourage underage drinking. He says that young people often believe that all college students engage in heavy drinking, but this is not true—*all* do not drink heavily or even drink at all. According to the NIAAA, in 2013 fewer than 13 percent of college students engaged in heavy drinking during the previous month and 39 percent had engaged in binge drinking. DeJong says that teens need to hear the truth about college drinking. They also need to know that laws are in place for a reason—and there is a price to pay for refusing to obey those laws. "Some people assume that students are so hell-bent on drinking, nothing can stop them. But it really is the case that enforcement works," says DeJong. He goes on to say, "Just because a law is commonly disobeyed doesn't mean we should eliminate it."[84]

> "Just because a law is commonly disobeyed doesn't mean we should eliminate it."[84]
>
> —William DeJong, a professor at Boston University's School of Public Health.

Parting Words from an Expert

Most people would agree that preventing alcohol abuse before it happens is much more sensible and precautionary than trying to fix the problem afterward. Strategies are in place in communities throughout the country, but experts say more needs to be done to curtail alcohol abuse. "We could alleviate a lot of human suffering and medical costs if we would address the problem of excessive alcohol use," says NIAAA director George Koob. "It's not something that's going away on its own, so we really need to be proactive."[85]

SOURCE NOTES

Chapter 1: The Nature of Alcohol Abuse

1. Quoted in Kim Painter, "Where America Drinks Most: Study Finds Binge-Drinking Trouble Spots," *USA Today*, April 24, 2015. www.usatoday.com.
2. Centers for Disease Control and Prevention, "Alcohol and Public Health: Frequently Asked Questions," July 9, 2015. www.cdc.gov.
3. Quoted in Julie Beck, "Anatomy of a Blackout," *Atlantic*, June 17, 2015. www.theatlantic.com.
4. Quoted in Maggie Fox, "Americans Are Drinking More—a Lot More," NBC News, April 23, 2015. www.nbcnews.com.
5. Quoted in Painter, "Where America Drinks Most."
6. Quoted in Kayla Blado, "Wisconsin Heaviest-Drinking State in Country," Wisconsin Public Radio, April 29, 2015. www.wpr.org.
7. Quoted in Andy Pierrotti and Terri Gruca, "Austin's Drinking Problem," KVUE, May 29, 2015. www.kvue.com.
8. Jeffrey M. Jones, "Drinking Highest Among Educated, Upper-Income Americans," Gallup, July 27, 2015. www.gallup.com.
9. Jones, "Drinking Highest Among Educated, Upper-Income Americans."
10. Quoted in Kendal Patterson, "Taking AIM at College Binge Drinking," Elements Behavioral Health, September 2015. www.elementsbehavioralhealth.com.
11. Quoted in Douglas Main, "30 Percent of Americans Have Had an Alcohol-Use Disorder," *Newsweek*, May 3, 2015. www.newsweek.com.
12. Quoted in Tyler Pager, "Underage Drinking, Binge Boozing by Minors Is on the Decline," *USA Today*, June 11, 2015. www.usatoday.com.
13. Child Trends, "Binge Drinking," August 2014. www.childtrends.org.

14. National Institute on Alcohol Abuse and Alcoholism, "College Drinking," October 2015. http://pubs.niaaa.nih.gov.
15. Ben Yeager, "What Happened When This College Student Drank Too Much, Too Quickly," *Washington Post*, August 31, 2015. www.washingtonpost.com.
16. Vince Calio, "States with the Most Drunk Driving," 24/7 Wall St., April 25, 2014. http://247wallst.com.

Chapter 2: What Are the Effects of Alcohol?

17. Rutgers University Student Health Services, "A Guide to Alcohol," 2011. http://healthservices.camden.rutgers.edu.
18. Rutgers University Student Health Services, "A Guide to Alcohol."
19. Sarah Hepola, *Blackout: Remembering the Things I Drank to Forget*. Boston: Grand Central, 2015.
20. Quoted in Hepola, *Blackout*.
21. Quoted in Beck, "Anatomy of a Blackout."
22. Quoted in Celia Vimont, "New Studies Shed Much-Needed Light on Alcohol-Induced Memory Blackouts," Partnership for Drug-Free Kids, June 15, 2012. www.drugfree.org.
23. Joshua Gowin, "Your Brain on Alcohol," *You, Illuminated* (blog), *Psychology Today*, June 18, 2010. www.psychology today.com.
24. Society for Neuroscience, "Neurotransmitters: How Brain Cells Use Chemicals to Communicate," BrainFacts, May 16, 2011. www.brainfacts.org.
25. National Institute on Alcohol Abuse and Alcoholism, *Beyond Hangovers*, October 2015. http://pubs.niaaa.nih.gov.
26. National Institute on Alcohol Abuse and Alcoholism, *Beyond Hangovers*.
27. Quoted in Tara Haelle, "Alcohol Can Rewire the Teenage Brain," *Science News for Students*, October 5, 2015. https://student.societyforscience.org.
28. Johns Hopkins Bloomberg School of Public Health, "Effects of Tobacco, Alcohol and Drugs on the Developing Adolescent Brain," *The Teen Years Explained*. www.jhsph.edu.
29. Quoted in Haelle, "Alcohol Can Rewire the Teenage Brain."

30. Lorena Siqueira and Vincent C. Smith, "Binge Drinking," *Pediatrics*, September 2015. http://pediatrics.aappublications .org.
31. Siqueira and Smith, "Binge Drinking."
32. National Institute on Alcohol Abuse and Alcoholism, "Alcohol Overdose: The Dangers of Drinking Too Much," October 2015. http://pubs.niaaa.nih.gov.
33. Quoted in Andrea Todd, "15 Shots of Vodka Killed Our Daughter," *Good Housekeeping*, October 13, 2015. www .goodhousekeeping.com.
34. American Liver Foundation, "Alcohol-Related Liver Disease," January 20, 2015. www.liverfoundation.org.
35. National Institute on Alcohol Abuse and Alcoholism, *Beyond Hangovers*.
36. National Institute on Alcohol Abuse and Alcoholism, *Beyond Hangovers*.

Chapter 3: How Addictive Is Alcohol?

37. Erica T., "What It's Really Like to Be a Young Female Alcoholic on the Way to Recovery," *Verily*, September 16, 2015. http:// verilymag.com.
38. Erica T., "What It's Really Like to Be a Young Female Alcoholic on the Way to Recovery."
39. Richard G. Soper, "Addiction: Character Defect or Chronic Disease?," *ASAM Magazine*, March 13, 2014. www.asam .org.
40. Barron H. Lerner, "Alcoholism Through a Doctor's Eyes," *Well* (blog), *New York Times*, February 13, 2014. http://well.blogs .nytimes.com.
41. National Council on Alcoholism and Drug Dependence, "Facts About Alcohol," July 25, 2015. https://ncadd.org.
42. National Institute on Alcohol Abuse and Alcoholism, "Neuroscience: Pathways to Alcohol Dependence," *Alcohol Alert*, April 2009. http://pubs.niaaa.nih.gov.
43. Quoted in Kristen McGuiness, "Alcoholism vs. Addiction," The Fix, September 22, 2011. www.thefix.com.
44. National Institute on Alcohol Abuse and Alcoholism, "Neuroscience."

45. National Council on Alcoholism and Drug Dependence, "Family History and Genetics," April 25, 2015. https://ncadd.org.

46. Quoted in Jennifer O'Brien, "Study Offers Clue as to Why Alcohol Is Addicting," University of California, San Francisco, January 11, 2012. www.ucsf.edu.

47. Quoted in O'Brien, "Study Offers Clue as to Why Alcohol Is Addicting."

48. American Psychological Association, "Understanding Alcohol Use Disorders & Their Treatment," March 2012. www.apa.org.

49. Erica T., "What It's Really Like to Be a Young Female Alcoholic on the Way to Recovery."

50. National Institute on Alcohol Abuse and Alcoholism, "A Family History of Alcoholism," June 2012. http://pubs.niaaa.nih.gov.

51. Therese J. Borchard, "Alcoholism & Depression: Frenemies Forever," *World of Psychology* (blog), PsychCentral, October 28, 2015. http://psychcentral.com.

52. David Sack, "Emotional Trauma: An Overlooked Root of Addiction," *Addiction Recovery* (blog), PsychCentral, May 2, 2012. http://blogs.psychcentral.com.

53. Joseph Nowinski, "Childhood Trauma and Alcohol Abuse: The Connection," *The Almost Effect* (blog), *Psychology Today*, July 29, 2013. www.psychologytoday.com.

Chapter 4: Treatment and Recovery Challenges

54. Lucy Rocca, "Being Teetotal Is Intoxicating: Giving Up Alcohol Gave Me Back My Life," *Guardian*, August 12, 2015. www.theguardian.com.

55. Quoted in Lisa Frederiksen, "Choosing Not to Drink—Meet Lucy Rocca," *BreakingTheCycles.com* (blog), March 12, 2014. www.breakingthecycles.com.

56. Rocca, "Being Teetotal Is Intoxicating."

57. Rocca, "Being Teetotal Is Intoxicating."

58. Elements Behavioral Health, "Dangerous Detox: Doing It at Home Could Be Deadly," September 15, 2011. www.elementsbehavioralhealth.com.

59. Jennifer Robinson, "Alcohol Withdrawal," WebMD Substance Abuse and Addiction Health Center, February 16, 2015. www.webmd.com.
60. Promises Treatment Centers, "What Happens During an Alcohol Detox and How Long Does It Last?," January 14, 2012. www.promises.com.
61. Promises Treatment Centers, "What Happens During an Alcohol Detox and How Long Does It Last?"
62. Joseph Goldberg, "Alcohol Detox Programs," WebMD Substance Abuse and Addiction Health Center, September 19, 2014. www.webmd.com.
63. Goldberg, "Alcohol Detox Programs."
64. Omar Manejwala, "How Often Do Long-Term Sober Alcoholics and Addicts Relapse?," *Craving* (blog), *Psychology Today*, February 13, 2014. www.psychologytoday.com.
65. American Psychological Association, "Understanding Alcohol Use Disorders & Their Treatment."
66. Quoted in *Good Morning America*, "'I Am. I Am an Alcoholic,' Says ABC News Anchor," January 24, 2014. http://abcnews.go.com.
67. Quoted in *Good Morning America*, "'I am. I Am an Alcoholic,' Says ABC News Anchor."
68. Lance Dodes, "The Pseudo-Science of Alcoholics Anonymous: There's a Better Way to Treat Addiction," *Salon*, March 23, 2014. www.salon.com.
69. Quoted in Jesse Singal, "Why Alcoholics Anonymous Works," *New York Magazine*, March 17, 2015. http://nymag.com.
70. National Institute on Alcohol Abuse and Alcoholism, "Treatment for Alcohol Problems: Finding and Getting Help," November 2014. http://pubs.niaaa.nih.gov.
71. Quoted in Gabrielle Glaser, "Could This Drug Cure Alcoholism?," *Daily Beast*, October 22, 2015. www.thedailybeast.com.

Chapter 5: How Can Alcohol Abuse Be Prevented?

72. Quoted in Elaine Korry, "To Prevent Addiction in Adults, Help Teens Learn How to Cope," NPR, November 13, 2015. www.npr.org.

73. Quoted in Korry, "To Prevent Addiction in Adults, Help Teens Learn How to Cope."
74. Quoted in Korry, "To Prevent Addiction in Adults, Help Teens Learn How to Cope."
75. Quoted in Korry, "To Prevent Addiction in Adults, Help Teens Learn How to Cope."
76. Quoted in Korry, "To Prevent Addiction in Adults, Help Teens Learn How to Cope."
77. Quoted in Laura Knudsen, "Youth Impact: High School Students Lead Substance Abuse Prevention Efforts," *Youth Today*, October 13, 2015. http://youthtoday.org.
78. Quoted in Elissa Rodriguez, "Every 15 Minutes Sends Powerful Message to High School Students," *Benito Link*, April 28, 2015. http://benitolink.com.
79. David Rosenbloom, "Workshop on Social Media, Web & Mobile Interventions for College Drinking," May 8, 2015. www.bu.edu.
80. Rosenbloom, "Workshop on Social Media, Web & Mobile Interventions for College Drinking."
81. Lisa Chedekel, "A New Approach to College Drinking," *BU Today*, August 4, 2015. www.bu.edu.
82. John M. McCardell, "Let Them Drink at 18, with a Learner's Permit," *Room for Debate* (blog), *New York Times*, May 28, 2012. www.nytimes.com.
83. William DeJong and Jason Blanchette, "Case Closed: Research Evidence on the Positive Public Health Impact of the Age 21 Minimum Legal Drinking Age in the United States," *Journal of Studies on Alcohol and Drugs*, February 2014. https://s3.amazonaws.com/s3.documentcloud.org/documents/1021584/drinkingagepaper.pdf.
84. Quoted in Boston University School of Public Health, "New Report on Minimum Drinking Age Makes Strong Case for Existing Laws," February 26, 2014. www.bu.edu.
85. Quoted in Steven Reinberg, "3 in 10 Americans Have Drinking Problem at Some Point in Their Lives," HealthDay, June 3, 2015. http://consumer.healthday.com.

ORGANIZATIONS TO CONTACT

Centers for Disease Control and Prevention (CDC)

1600 Clifton Rd.
Atlanta, GA 30329
phone: (800) 232-4636
website: www.cdc.gov

America's leading health protection agency, the CDC seeks to promote health and quality of life by controlling disease, injury, and disability. Its website features numerous articles, fact sheets, and policy statements about alcohol abuse and alcoholism.

Community Anti-Drug Coalitions of America (CADCA)

625 Slaters Ln., Suite 300
Alexandria, VA 22314
phone: (800) 542-2322 • fax (703) 706-0565
website: www.cadca.org

Through its network of more than five thousand local coalitions, the CADCA brings together community leaders to address a variety of issues from underage drinking to drug abuse. The website's offerings include a resources and research section, an interactive media section, and a search engine that produces a number of articles about alcohol abuse, treatment, and prevention.

Foundation for a Drug-Free World

1626 N. Wilcox Ave., Suite 1297
Los Angeles, CA 90028
phone: (818) 952-5260; toll-free: (888) 668-6378
e-mail: info@drugfreeworld.org • website: www.drugfreeworld.org

The Foundation for a Drug-Free World exists to empower young people with facts about drugs so they can make good decisions and live drug-free. A wealth of information about drugs and alcohol can be found on the interactive website, including an informative booklet called *The Truth About Alcohol*.

Foundation for Advancing Alcohol Responsibility (Responsibility.org)

2345 Crystal Dr., Suite 710
Arlington, VA 22202
phone: (202) 637-0077
website: http://responsibility.org

Responsibility.org seeks to eliminate underage drinking and drunk driving while promoting responsible decision making about alcohol. Its website has separate sections related to drunk driving, underage alcohol use, and binge drinking; a news and resources area with additional articles about teenage drinking; and a link to the foundation's blog.

National Council on Alcoholism and Drug Dependence (NCADD)

217 Broadway, Suite 712
New York, NY 10007
phone: (212) 269-7797 • fax: (212) 269-7510
e-mail: national@ncadd.org • website: http://ncadd.org

The NCADD is a leading advocacy organization whose focus is addressing alcoholism and drug dependence. Its website offers a wealth of informative articles, statistics, fact sheets, booklets, and other publications about alcohol abuse and alcoholism.

National Institute on Alcohol Abuse and Alcoholism (NIAAA)

5635 Fishers Ln., MSC 9304
Bethesda, MD 20892
phone: (301) 443-3860

e-mail: niaaaweb-r@exchange.nih.gov
website: www.niaaa.nih.gov

An agency of the National Institutes of Health, the NIAAA is the lead federal agency for research on alcohol use and abuse. Its website features brochures, research updates, news articles, fact sheets, classroom resources, and videos.

National Institute on Drug Abuse (NIDA)

National Institutes of Health
6001 Executive Blvd., Room 5213
Bethesda, MD 20892
phone: (301) 443-1124
e-mail: information@nida.nih.gov • website: www.drugabuse.gov

NIDA supports research efforts and ensures the rapid dissemination of research to improve drug abuse prevention, treatment, and policy. The website links to a separate NIDA for Teens site (https://teens.drugabuse.gov/), which provides a great deal of information for teens about drugs and alcohol.

Office of Adolescent Health (OAH)

1101 Wootton Pkwy., Suite 700
Rockville, MD 20852
phone: (240) 453-2846
e-mail: oah.gov@hhs.gov • website: www.hhs.gov/ash/oah

An agency of the US Department of Health and Human Services, the OAH is dedicated to improving the health and well-being of adolescents. Its website has an adolescent health section that contains a wide variety of articles, fact sheets, and other information specifically for teens about health and nutrition, mental health, and substance abuse.

Office of National Drug Control Policy

750 Seventeenth St. NW
Washington, DC 20503
phone: (800) 666-3332 • fax: (202) 395-6708
e-mail: ondcp@ncjrs.org • website: www.whitehouse.gov/ondcp

A component of the Executive Office of the President, the Office of National Drug Control Policy is responsible for directing the federal government's antidrug programs. A search engine produces a number of publications about alcohol abuse.

Partnership for Drug-Free Kids

352 Park Ave. S., 9th Floor
New York, NY 10010
phone: (212) 922-1560 • fax: (212) 922-1570
website: www.drugfree.org

The Partnership for Drug-Free Kids is dedicated to helping parents and families solve the teenage substance abuse problem. Its website offers numerous fact sheets, reports, and other publications about alcohol abuse.

Students Against Destructive Decisions (SADD)

255 Main St.
Marlborough, MA 01752
phone: (877) 723-3462
website: www.sadd.org/contact-sadd

Formerly Students Against Drunk Driving, SADD seeks to empower young people to successfully confront substance abuse and the other risks and pressures that challenge them in their daily lives. A number of articles, videos, news releases, newsletters, and other communications are available through the website.

Substance Abuse and Mental Health Services Administration (SAMHSA)

1 Choke Cherry Rd.
Rockville, MD 20857
phone: (877) 726-4727 • fax: (240) 221-4292
e-mail: SAMHSAInfo@samhsa.hhs.gov
website: www.samhsa.gov

SAMHSA's mission is to reduce the impact of substance abuse and mental illness on America's communities. The site offers a wealth of information about alcohol and alcoholism.

FOR FURTHER RESEARCH

Books

Susan Cheever, *Drinking in America: Our Secret History*. New York: Twelve, 2015.

Sarah Hepola, *Blackout: Remembering the Things I Drank to Forget*. Boston: Grand Central, 2015.

Marc Lewis, *The Biology of Desire: Why Addiction Is Not a Disease*. New York: PublicAffairs, 2015.

Terry Teague Meyer, *I Have an Alcoholic Parent. Now What?* New York: Rosen, 2015.

Mount Mercy College, *Teens Affected by Addiction: Stories and Advice from People Who Have Grown Up with an Addict.* Seattle: Amazon Digital Services, 2015. Kindle edition.

Gail Stewart, *Teens and Drinking*. San Diego: ReferencePoint, 2015.

Internet Sources

American Academy of Pediatrics, "AAP Warns of the Dangers of Binge Drinking in Adolescents," August 31, 2015. www.aap .org/en-us/about-the-aap/aap-press-room/pages/AAP-Warns -of-the-Dangers-of-Binge-Drinking-in-Adolescents.aspx.

Kathryn Doyle, "Teens Exposed to Alcohol Use in Films Were Most Likely to Have Tried It, Too," Huffington Post, June 17, 2015. www .huffingtonpost.com/2015/04/17/teen-alcohol-film_n_7080170 .html.

Gabrielle Glaser, "The Irrationality of Alcoholics Anonymous," *Atlantic*, April 2015. www.theatlantic.com/magazine /archive/2015/04/the-irrationality-of-alcoholics-anonymous /386255.

Tara Haelle, "Alcohol Can Rewire the Teenage Brain," Science News for Students, October 5, 2015. https://student.societyfor science.org/article/alcohol-can-rewire-teenage-brain.

John Hill, "The Rehab Racket: The Way We Treat Addiction Is a Costly, Dangerous Mess," *Mother Jones*, June 2015. www .motherjones.com/politics/2015/05/ryan-rogers-rehab-alcoholic -drugged.

Kimberly Leonard, "The Dangers of 'Overage' Drinking," *US News & World Report*, May 13, 2015. www.usnews.com/news /articles/2015/05/13/alcohol-abuse-among-older-population-a -cause-for-concern.

National Institute on Alcohol Abuse and Alcoholism, "Alcohol Overdose: The Dangers of Drinking Too Much," October 2015. http://pubs.niaaa.nih.gov/publications/AlcoholOverdoseFact sheet/Overdosefact.htm.

Samantha Olson, "Teen Binge Drinking Damages the Brain: How Partying Affects Learning and Memory Forever," Medical Daily, April 27, 2015. www.medicaldaily.com/teen-binge-drinking-dam ages-brain-how-partying-affects-learning-and-memory-forever -330898.

Maanvi Singh, "Teens Who Skimp on Sleep Now Have More Drinking Problems Later," NPR, January 16, 2015. www.npr .org/sections/health-shots/2015/01/16/377720744/teens-who -skimp-on-sleep-now-have-more-drinking-problems-later.

Dennis Thompson, "Many Teens Knowingly Ride with Drunk Drivers, Survey Finds," HealthDay, October 22, 2015. http://consum er.healthday.com/kids-health-information-23/adolescents-and -teen-health-news-719/teens-and-drunk-drivers-704526.html.

Websites

The Cool Spot (www.thecoolspot.gov). A product of the National Institute on Alcohol Abuse and Alcoholism, this site was created to help teens better understand the effects of alcohol, the risks of drinking at a young age, and how to handle peer pressure, among other facts related to drinking.

DoSomething.org (www.dosomething.org). A nonprofit organization focused on social change, DoSomething.org recruits young people to get involved and take action through national campaigns and project grants. Available on the website are facts about alcohol abuse and teens and alcohol as well as a "Designated Texter" game and other features related to alcohol abuse.

Every 15 Minutes (www.everyfifteenminutes.org). The official website of the Every 15 Minutes program, which is conducted for teenagers and families around the world. This site serves as a central hub for the exchange of information concerning the program.

Too Smart to Start (www.toosmarttostart.samhsa.gov/teens). A product of the Substance Abuse and Mental Health Services Administration, Too Smart to Start is designed for teenagers to help them avoid using alcohol.

INDEX

Note: Boldface page numbers indicate illustrations.

Acamprosate, 51
adolescent(s)
  brain, and response to alcohol, 20–22
  past month alcohol use/binge drinking
    among, **13**
  perils of drinking by, 23–24
  prevalence of AUD among, 12
  prevalence of drunk driving among, 11
alcohol (ethanol)
  effects of, on driving skills, 21
  levels of, in standard drinks, 5
alcohol addiction/alcoholism, 29–31
  brain changes associated with, 32–33
  change in attitudes about, 30
  childhood trauma and, 38–39
  genetics and, 35–36, 37
  mental health disorders and, 36–38
  percentage of Americans seeking
    treatment for, **45**
  See also prevention; treatment(s)
alcohol consumption
  demographic disparities in, 8–9
  gender and recommendations for, 5
  moderate, benefits of, 27
  prevalence among US adults, 4
  regional variations in, 7–8
alcohol dehydrogenase, 5
alcohol poisoning, 24–26
alcohol use disorder (AUD), 10–11
  See also alcohol addiction/alcoholism
Alcoholics Anonymous (AA), 30, 47–50,
  49
American Journal of Public Health, 4
American Liver Foundation, 26, 27
American Psychiatric Association (APA),
  10
American Psychological Association, 35
Amethyst Initiative, 60
AUD. *See* alcohol use disorder
Austin, TX, 7–8

Big Book of Alcoholics Anonymous, 47
binge drinking
  among college students, 12–13
  definition of, 5
  drinking age and, 61–62
  increase in, 6
Blackout (Hepola), 17
blackouts (alcohol-induced amnesia),
  16–17, 19
Blanchette, Jason, 62
blood alcohol concentration (BAC)
  from binge drinking, 5
  effects of, by level, **18**
Borchard, Therese J., 37–38
brain, **23**
  adolescent, and response to alcohol,
    20–22
  alcohol and chemistry of, 19–20,
    34–35
  changes in, associated with alcohol
    addiction, 32–33
breast cancer, 28

Calio, Vince, 15
cancers, 28
cardiomyopathy, alcoholic, 28
Centers for Disease Control and
  Prevention (CDC), 70
  on alcohol levels in standard drinks, 5
  on deaths from alcohol poisoning, 26
  on drinking and driving, 14–15
  on percentage of teens having driven
    after drinking, 11
Child Trends, 12
Choice program, 55
Christian, Claudia, 51
cirrhosis, 27
cognitive-behavioral therapy, 46
Community Anti-Drug Coalitions of
  America (CADCA), 70
Constitution, US. *See* Eighteenth
  Amendment; Twenty-Sixth
  Amendment

D'Amico, Elizabeth, 54–55
deaths
    from alcohol poisoning, 26
    from alcohol-related car crashes, 21
DeJong, William, 62
delirium tremens (DTs), 42, 43
depression, 36–38
detox, 41–43
Disulfiram, 51
drinking age
    debate over, 60–62
    support for lowering, **61**
Driver, Rita K., 43
driving under the influence (DUI), 21
    prevalence of, among youth, 11

Ehlers, Cindy L., 32
Eighteenth Amendment, 58
Elements Behavioral Health, 42
endorphins, 34–35
Ernest Gallo Clinic and Research
    Center (University of California, San
    Francisco), 34
Every 15 Minutes program, 56–58

Firewater Myth, 32
Foundation for a Drug-Free World, 70–71
Foundation for Advancing Alcohol
    Responsibility, 71
Foundation for the Advancement of
    Alcohol Responsibility, 15

gamma-aminobutyric acid (GABA), 20
gender
    prevalence of drinking and, 9
    recommendations for alcohol
        consumption based on, 5
genetics, 32, 35–36
    eye color associated with alcoholism
        and, 37
Gizer, Ian R., 32
glutamate, 20
Goldberg, Joseph, 44–45
Gowin, Joshua, 19
Greenfield, Shelly, 36

Harvard T.H. Chan School of Public
    Health, 27
heart, 28
heavy drinking

definition of, 5
health risks of, 28
increase in, 6
industries/occupations associated
    with, 14
See also alcohol addiction/alcoholism
hepatitis, alcoholic, 26–27
Hepola, Sarah, 17
Hietpas, Diane, 7

Institute for Health Metrics and Evaluation
    (IHME), 4, 6
    on regional variations in alcohol use, 7

Janda, Alexis, 26
Johns Hopkins Bloomberg School of
    Public Health, 22
Jones, Jeffrey M., 9

Knight, John, 52, 54
Koob, George, 6, 10, 63

Lange, Riley, 58
Lerner, Barron H., 30
Levy, Sharon, 53
Li, Dawei, 37
liver, 26–27
Lucey, Rich, 12

Manejwala, Omar, 45–46
McCardell, John M., 60–62
Menominee Indian Reservation, 7
met-enkephalin, **34**
Minimum Drinking Age Act (1984), 60, 62
Mitchell, Bob, 7–8
Mitchell, Jennifer, 35
Mokdad, Ali, 4, 5
Monitoring the Future (MTF) survey, 12,
    55
Mother Jones (magazine), 44
Mothers Against Drunk Driving (MADD),
    11, 54
motivational enhancement therapy, 46

Naltrexone, 51
National Council on Alcoholism and Drug
    Dependence (NCADD), 21, 30–31, 33,
    71
National Highway Traffic Safety
    Administration (NHTSA), 15

National Institute on Alcohol Abuse and
    Alcoholism (NIAAA), 4, 10, 71–72
    on alcohol poisoning, 24
    on alcohol use disorder, 11
    on alcoholism and genetics, 36
    on blackouts, 17
    on health risks of heavy drinking, 28
    on medication-assisted treatments,
        50–51
    on motivational enhancement therapy,
        46
National Institute on Drug Abuse (NIDA),
    12, 72
Native Americans, 32
Nelson, Naja, 56
neurotransmitters, 20
    excitatory vs. inhibitory, 19
New York Times (newspaper), 61
Nowinski, Joseph, 39

Office of Adolescent Health (US
    Department of Health and Human
    Services), 72
Office of National Drug Control Policy,
    72–73
opinion polls. *See* surveys

Partnership for Drug-Free Kids, 73
Phillips, Dave, 11
polls. *See* surveys
post-acute withdrawal syndrome
    (PAWS), 50
prevention
    by peer groups, 55–56
    with programs targeting substance
        abuse at early age, 52–55
    with shock programs, 56–58
    strategies for colleges, 59–60
Prohibition, 58, 60
Promises Treatment Centers, 43

race/ethnicity, prevalence of drinking
    and, 9
Risher, Mary-Louise, 22
Robinson, Jennifer, 43
Rocca, Lucy, 40–41
Rosenbloom, David, 59, 60
Rutgers University, 16

Sack, David, 38, 50

Screening, Brief Intervention, and Referral
    to Treatment (SBIRT) program, 52–53
Sharp, John, 33
Sherman, Julia, 7
Siqueira, Lorena, 20–21, 23
Smith, Vincent C., 23
Society for Neuroscience, 19
Soper, Richard G., 30
states
    having worst problems with drunk
        driving, 15
    variations in alcohol use among, 7–8
steatosis (fatty liver), 26
Students Against Destructive Decisions
    (SADD), 73
Substance Abuse and Mental Health
    Services Administration (SAMHSA),
    11–12, 14, 36, 73
Sulovari, Arvis, 37
surveys
    on alcohol consumption among US
        adults, 8–9
    on alcohol use among youth, 12
    on lowering drinking age to 18, **61**
Szalavitz, Maia, 32

Thornton, Mark, 58
treatment(s)
    barriers to, 43–44
    inpatient, 44
    outpatient, 44–45
    percentage of Americans seeking, **45**
    psychotherapy, 46–47
    twelve-step approach, 47–50
triglycerides, 26
twelve-step programs, 47–50
Twenty-Sixth Amendment, 60

Vargas, Elizabeth, 46–47

White, Aaron, 5, 17
Wisconsin, 7
withdrawal, alcohol, symptoms of, 20,
    42–43
women
    increase in binge/heavy drinking by, 6
    metabolism of alcohol in, 5

Yeager, Ben, 13–14, 15
Youth Advisory Board (YAB), 55

PICTURE CREDITS